Russian Poetry under the Tsars

Russian Poetry

An Anthology

under the Tsars

Translated, and with an
Introduction and Notes,
by Burton Raffel

State University of New York Press, Albany, 1971

Published by State University of New York Press
Thurlow Terrace, Albany, New York 12201

© 1971 State University of New York

ISBN 0 – 87395 – 070 – 4 (clothbound)
ISBN 0 – 87395 – 170 – 0 (microfiche)
Library of Congress Catalog Card Number 74 – 136279
Printed in the United States of America

Designed by Richard Hendel

To the memory of my father,

HARRY L. RAFFEL,

born in Bardechev, the Ukraine

But poetry united us all. In Yaroslavl [prison]
I had often thought that I alone sought and found
in it a way out of the closed circle of my life, that
only I was visited by Alexander Blok in my
dungeon, only I repeated to myself on my solitary
walks: "If I am to be poisoned, let it be by poetry."
This was a conceited illusion, I now discovered, as
I listened to the floods of verse we poured out,
our own and other people's, simple or
sophisticated, lyrical or sardonic.

EVGENIA S. GINZBURG, *Into the Whirlwind*

Contents

Introduction

RUSSIAN POETRY (and also Russian prose) has a curve very much shorter, and distinctly steeper, than that of poetry in any comparable European culture. "English meter," notes Vladimir Nabokov, "came into being almost four centuries before Russian meter did" (*Notes on Prosody*, p. 51). The long period of absorption of classical influences, so common in Western literatures, does not exist in Russian literary history: classical influences swept in, virtually all at once, in the general tidal wave blown up by Tsar Peter the Great (1672–1725). The long age of chivalry, the Renaissance—nothing of this exists in Russian literary history. The growth of Russian literature has been compared to a hypothetical English literature in which, after the Anglo-Saxon Chronicles and *Beowulf*, suddenly there came Dryden, Pope, and Johnson.

All cultures of course have literature. The point is, however, that Russian poetry, like the culture which grew it, suffered long centuries of enfeeblement. Beginning as an offshoot of Christian Byzantium, toward the end of the tenth century, Russian culture was subject to a rigorous antisecularism and, more seriously, to the immense disturbances created by Tartar invasion and conquest. Vladimir Monomakh, Grand Prince of Kiev from 1113 to 1125, was himself a writer of considerable skill; Dmitri Donskoy, who in 1389 began the process of pushing back the Tartars, was barely able to sign his own name. Cultural continuity was broken off so sharply that the late twelfth-century *Song of Igor's Campaign* lay buried until the late eighteenth century and, when finally rediscovered, was so incomprehensible an achievement that for many years scholars doubted (and some still doubt) its authenticity. Almost certainly genuine, it remains in a kind of splendid isolation, with nothing before it, nothing after it, to explain how or by whom it was produced. *Beowulf* is the sole surviving Old English epic—but a good many other Old English poems have survived along with *Beowulf*, and from them, as well as from other sources, we can tell a great deal about the culture which created the poetry. No comparable reconstruction is ever likely to be made for the *Song of Igor's Campaign* (a fine and complex work, badly mauled in Vladimir Nabokov's 1960 translation; see the more recent version by Sidney Monas and myself in *Delos*, no. 6).

Folk poetry, both religious and secular, did exist, and much of it has been preserved, as it was composed, by oral repetition. (Oral transmission is deeply conservative; centuries of repeated recitation and rememorization do not usually drastically distort the original version.) Because nineteenth-century Russian scholars began to notice, and to record, and because later poets began to make use of this poetry, I have included two outstanding samples, in section 1 of this book: for a brief discussion, see page 3. But although, from Lermontov to the Soviet period, poets have imitated the older oral verse, it is of virtually no importance in the genesis of Russian poetry, neither technically nor in its subject matter. Russian poetry was an exclusively lettered creation; it was written for, and often written by, the increasingly Westernized aristocracy created by the furious, cruel, and astonishingly effective reforms of Peter the Great. Gavrila Derzhavin (1743–1816) is by universal agreement "the first real poet in Russia" (the words are Nabokov's, *Notes on Prosody*, p. 43); the metrical reforms which made his work possible do not predate him by so much as half a century.

Russian poetry begins, then, in about the middle of the eighteenth century, when a workable prosody was first evolved. That prosody has a confused and improbable history. Formal verse became re-established in Russia in about the seventeenth century—crude, rather doggerel-like stuff that might have struggled into better things but was killed off by the influence of the neighboring Polish culture, already well in advance of that in Russia. (The White Russian monk, Simeon of Polotsk [1629–1680], was the primary importer of the alien form, which stultified Russian verse for over a century.) Polish and Russian are of course very close, in many ways, but their intonation is basically dissimilar: Polish has a fixed stress, which falls always on the next-to-last syllable in a word. This results in a comparative weakening of stress: that is, in a language where stress is predictable, like Polish, it cannot be used to distinguish one word from another. Even though it is predictable and of weakened linguistic weight, stress of course still exists in Polish, but not as meaningfully as in languages like Russian, or English, where stress is free and can occur at any point in a word. In Russian and in English, shifts in stress may be the only means of distinguishing one word from another: in English, for example, "content" and "content" are orthographically and etymologically identical, but one is a noun meaning "that which is contained inside a thing," and the other is an adjective meaning "pleased, satisfied." We know one word from the other chiefly by the difference in stress: CON-tent is the noun, and con-TENT is the adjective.

Rhythm is the basis of poetry; a basic difference in intonation tends to make for a basic difference in prosody. Polish stress being of almost no linguistic utility, syntactically or lexically, it tends to be of no great significance in the prosody of the language, which thus relies on a syllabic rather than an accentual measure—i.e., Polish measures a poetic line simply by the number of syllables in it, ignoring both the number and the position of accented syllables. The Polish line imported into Russian verse, accordingly, is a basic measure of thirteen syllables, broken by a caesura after the seventh syllable. How deeply unsuited this was for Russian, as it would be for English (though there are poets, from time to time, who pretend to be writing syllabic poetry in English), can perhaps be seen by taking an iambic pentameter line of Shakespeare's, and rewriting it to something like the Polish type of syllabic measure:

That time of year thou mayst in me behold . . .

This euphonious line exhibits, unfortunately, only ten syllables. Three need to be added—and the caesura brought into lumbering being:

That season of passing year thou mayst in me behold . . .

The effect on Russian poetry was predictably disastrous. "Unendurable dullness settles upon him who peruses these imitations of structures, mediocre in themselves and completely alien to the rhythm of live Russian" (ibid., p. 35). Two eighteenth-century poets rebelled against this straitjacketing of Russian. Vasily K. Trediakovsky (1703–1769) began the shift to what is now called "syllabo-tonic" verse (I will explain the term in a moment); Mikhail V. Lomonosov (1711–1765) essentially completed the process. Recognizing the vital importance of stress in Russian, these reformers pointed out that verse could be made to conform to natural facts just as well as to an artificial syllabic measure. In iambic verse, that is, syllables are still important; an iambic foot requires precisely two syllables, not one or seven or fourteen; an iambic line, composed of a specified number of iambic feet, similarly requires a fixed number of syllables. *But*, the point was now made, it is the alternation of *stressed and unstressed* syllables, rather than the mere stringing together of a certain *quantity* of syllables, that made the most effective Russian verse. In effect, then, "syllabo-tonic" verse takes its name from a historical-semantic situation peculiar to Russian, and need not concern us as a critical label. Russian metrics are of course not identical to English metrics, but for my purposes here no further distinctions need be drawn.

"Prosody begins to matter only after poets have started to use it," says Nabokov very neatly (ibid., p. 35), and until the latter part of the eighteenth century Russian culture had not produced real poets. Much groundwork had still to be done. Translations of Western books, at Peter's direction in the beginning, but afterwards by processes more and more natural, began to pour into Russians' hands. French literature, in particular, became enormously influential: much of early Russian poetry consists of sterile imitations drawn from French models. The significant fact is that these imitations had important social functions: success at even this barren form of Russian poetry was a distinct social asset, and careers (Derzhavin's among them) could be made by flattering odes and epistles. As for prosody: many poems originally written and published in the Polish technique, including Trediakovsky's, were twenty or twenty-five years later rewritten in iambics. By Derzhavin's time the syllabic metric was effectively dead.

Nineteenth-century critics saw a sharp, clear break between the poetry of the eighteenth century—which they saw as overwhelmingly crude, pioneering stuff—and the immensely sophisticated and subtle poetic culture which produced Pushkin and the other poets of the so-called Golden Age. It is now recognized that the eighteenth-century writers did more than simply pioneer: their achievement was directly and often substantially influential on their poetic descendants, and it was a respectable achievement in its own right. Sumarokov and Khemnitser are often graceful writers; Derzhavin tends to be a bit lumbering, but his work is clearly his own, and his independence of mind led him to important breaks with neoclassical tradition. Krylov is a master—one of the first Russian poets to be of importance more for his own sake than for his historical place in the development of Russian literature. Zhukovsky and Batyushkov, the last of the pre-Pushkin poets here translated, are again both masters. Like Krylov, Zhukovsky's range is not great, but what he does, he does beautifully, sometimes superbly. And Batyushkov is, on a smaller, thinner scale, almost an early Pushkin; he anticipates a very great deal, and remains immensely readable. In short, if it would be fatuous to say that Russia was ready for Pushkin, it is at least fair to say that Russian poetry had achieved enough, by the time Pushkin began to write, so that he stands in a historical line. He is an overwhelming figure, he remade and redirected all of Russian literature: his mark is still on it; his influence is still vital—probably more vital than, say, Dante's or Shakespeare's in either Italian or English literature. But one can also see where Pushkin came from, and the shoulders on which he stands.

I have tried to indicate something of Pushkin's particular place in Russian society in the biographical note introducing the translations of his poems, later in this book. Something needs to be said about that society in general—though I cannot do more, here, than emphasize the grossest highlights of a complex and changing picture. Basically, Russian society in modern times—roughly, from the time of Peter the Great to today—has been repressive; it has also tended toward autocracy. But the downward pressure of the controlling forces has not been steady: it is remarkable how variable those pressures have been, at one period permitting excited, expansive feelings of liberation, while at another period bearing down so savagely that culture and hope seemed to die together. This has not been a deliberate variation, though it has been pretty much cyclical. Rather, it is the only way in which autocracy can in fact manage to find a social balance. The veering back and forth, the pushing and pulling between allowing the governed greater ranges of expression, or denying them even previously permitted ranges—all this is an essential social dynamic. It is the inevitable process by which a society such as Russia adjusts itself to upward pressures, pressures not initiated by nor directly in the control of the relatively small governing class.

I have said that Russia has always *tended* toward autocracy, and also that its basic dynamic was, *tout court*, that of an out-and-out autocracy. Both statements are, I think, true. The Russian autocracy of the Tsars, and the later autocracy of the Bolsheviks, has never achieved full, ideal "oriental" efficiency; Russian society has always had cracks and flaws in its repressive apparatus. (Compare Wittfogel's *Oriental Despotism*, a vastly stimulating discussion.) From the standpoint of America, or of England, this may not seem particularly relevant: the cruel accomplishments of even a partially defective autocracy seem, from this liberal-democratic perspective, so horrifying that the fissures and flaws fade into insignificance. Avrahm Yarmolinsky writes, for example (viewing things Russian from the Anglo-American perspective I have just mentioned), about the "white terror" of 1848:

> The schools too were subjected to new stringencies. The universities were ordered to base their teachings not on rational but on religious truths, and the rectors and deans were enjoined to see to it that nothing in the instruction favored socialism or communism. The chair of philosophy was abolished on the ground that the subject, while not demonstrably useless, was possibly harmful. All thought of reform, particularly the freedom of the serfs, was abandoned. The

country breathed an intolerably oppressive air. (*Road to Revolution*, p. 84)

This is true, and yet somehow also false. Thirteen years after this period of undoubtedly severe repression, the serfs were in fact freed—an immensely significant step, dreamed about by Russian radicals for a very long time. "All thought" of reform *cannot* have been extinguished, when in little more than a decade so basic a reform was achieved. Yes, it can be argued, but this is the cyclical veering back and forth of which I spoke a moment ago. It is that, of course, but it is also the fact that "intolerably oppressive" is not and, at least in the Russian context, cannot be understood to be absolute. Repression is always intolerable, and yet always bearable, except to those on whom it happens to fall most directly, immediately—and so unbearably. At the same time, however, the repressed go on thinking of, and as they can working toward, some state of lesser repression. This was possible even in the infinitely more efficient autocracy of Hitler's Germany, though not to anything like the same degree; Mussolini's Italy would be perhaps a more accurate parallel. The famous reading circle of which Dostoyevsky was a member, and for participation in which he was first subjected to a mock execution and was then exiled to Siberia, was active in exactly the period Yarmolinsky describes; Dostoyevsky was arrested and sentenced in 1849. Richard Hare seems to me to have a more delicate feeling for the full truth of life in Tsarist Russia's autocracy: "No wonder that a haunting sense of instability pervaded every layer of this complex and unprecedented society. The spiritual bonds uniting the upper strata with the lower ones were tenuous and strained; the rift between them was slowly but surely widening" (*Pioneers of Russian Social Thought*, pp. 3–4). Hare is also very clear about the effect of Tsarist repression on Pushkin and his friends:

> When Nicholas I suppressed the amateur military revolt [of The Decembrists] ... he simultaneously crippled the independent-minded, energetic and gifted aristocracy of early nineteenth-century Russia. Their *élan*, enterprise and exuber-

ant originality, finding no broad constructive outlet, ran wild or sank into paralysis. . . . The brilliant European-minded generation of Pushkin took refuge in agriculture, in dissipation, or in the freer but more exacting sphere of the arts, where several proved to be supreme. The unwieldy Empire began to wilt under the exasperating control of civil servants and policemen. (Ibid., pp. 7–8)

Another, more subjective way of putting this was formulated in the 1840s by the immensely influential Russian critic, Vissarion Belinsky: "The poet receives his substance from the life of his nation; consequently, the merits, depth, scope, and importance of that substance depend directly and immediately upon the historical importance of his nation's life and not upon the poet himself or his talent" ("Thoughts and Notes on Russian Literature," in *Belinsky, Chernyshevsky, and Dobrolyubov: Selected Criticism*, p. 15). Valid, perhaps, only for nations capable of "historical importance," this is nevertheless a typical Russian perspective.

The poets who follow Pushkin, then, lived through three-quarters of a century in which the Tsarist Empire slowly crumbled, gradually rotted. (The characters of Chekhov's stories and plays show that rot at very nearly its apogee; see also the protagonist of Goncharov's too little known novel, *Oblomov*.) The process is already operating in Lermontov, only fifteen years Pushkin's junior and dead a bare four years after him. Even in Pushkin's grim *The Bronze Horseman* there is a sense of at least the possibility of hope. Not in Lermontov: "Life/has nothing to give, had nothing/to give: And all I need/is nothingness, its freedom, its peace." Tyutchev and Fet, the two major poets of the second half of the nineteenth century, are both primarily lyricists—and both were also reactionaries in politics. Tyutchev actually worked as a government censor (as did Polonsky, another poet of this same period). Russian poetry makes no huge steps forward from Tyutchev to Fet; "the life of the nation," to paraphrase Belinsky, did not encourage such leaps. Yet there are not only these strong, individual, and often singularly beautiful voices, expanding and deepening Pushkin's heritage, but there are also poets like Pavlova, A. K. Tolstoy, Polonsky, and Sluchevsky—minor poets, but good minor poets, eclectic talents capable of writing first-rate verse. They have only to be compared with Sumarokov, Khemnitser, and even Derzhavin, to see how far the general level of Russian poetry had moved, in only a century. And there were others, notably Nikolai Andreyevitch Nekrasov (1821–1877). The last half of the nineteenth century may be a doldrums in Russian poetry, but again, this is a strictly relative classification.

The alienation of which Richard Hare spoke, above, grew acute toward the end of the century, culminating in a swift succession of literary movements—Symbolism, Acmeism, Futurism—the first and third of which express a basic rejection of accepted ways; the second of which attempts to affirm what positive values it can find in the contemporary order of things. Symbolism, much influenced by French Symbolist poets (Baudelaire, Verlaine, Rimbaud, Mallarmé), is perhaps best identifiable, in its Russian incarnation, as an attempt to keep artistically extraneous matters from dominating art. Oleg Maslenikov, in a brief but extremely clear discussion, notes that Russian Symbolism "had its beginnings in the protest against the utilitarian demands with which Russian critics traditionally saddled literature. It first came as an apology for 'art for art's sake.' . . . The Symbolists were first and foremost individualists" ("Russian Literature from 1890–1917," in *A Handbook of Slavic Studies*, p. 440). Russian Symbolism emphasizes, as did Symbolism in France and elsewhere, the individual imagination, the necessity for craftsmanship of a superlatively high order, and it attempts to deal with life by literary indirections, by "symbols." Tyutchev and Fet are predecessors of the Symbolists; Vladimir Sergeyevitch Soloviev (1853–1900) is a precursor and a major influence (especially on Blok), and Annensky is a kind of cognate development, allied but separate. Valery Yakovlevitch Bryusov (1873–1924) was the leading figure of the early Symbolists, together with Balmont and Sologub (though they were superior to him as poets). They were followed by Andrey Biely (1880–

1921), best known in the West as a novelist; by the greatest of twentieth-century Russian poets, Blok; and finally by a poet whose major work places him outside the time-span covered by this book, Vyacheslov Ivanovitch Ivanov (1866–1949).

But the indirections of Symbolism came to seem excessive— were at times excessive. Acmeism, a transient movement upheld by three main figures—Gumilev, Akhmatova, and Mandelstam— was actually begun by the relatively minor poet, Mikhail Kuzmin, with his 1910 manifesto, "Concerning Beautiful Clarity." The Acmeists rejected the vagueness and esotericism of Symbolism: it was *this* world they wanted to write about, and in the most precise, the firmest-etched terms. Their principal organ, the journal *Apollon*, takes its name from the notion of Apollonian clarity (as opposed to Dionysian frenzy: see Spengler's *The Decline of the West*). The Acmeists insisted, in a sense, on words-for-meaning's-sake, rather than on words-for-music's-sake, which had come to be associated with much Symbolist work. Restrained, more classical than Romantic, Acmeist verse inevitably tends to focus on what words can in fact describe and analyze, rather than on what slips and slides away from verbal expression; the emphasis is thus on external events instead of on internal ones. And mystical expression has very little place: Akhmatova's terse, brief, colloquial and conversational early poems, several of which are here translated, are perhaps typical of the movement at its best.

Symbolism could linger on, in the person of Ivanov and also as a major and continuing influence. Acmeism was effectively killed off by the Revolution. For the most part it came to seem, as Trotsky scornfully put it, simply irrelevant. "The poets, uncalled to the holy sacrifice, proved themselves, as was to be expected, the most insignificant of all insignificant children of the earth. Symbolists, Parnassians, Acmeists, who had flown above social interests and passions, as if in the clouds, found themselves in Ekaterinodar with the Whites...." (Leon Trotsky, *Literature and Revolution*, p. 23). Futurism, though it had its birth before the Revolution, was not to fully develop until afterwards, in the work, especially, of Mayakovsky, and to a degree, also, of Esenin, both of them outside the scope of this book. The Futurists' first manifesto, in 1912, was entitled *A Slap in the Face of Public Taste*, and called for an end to all traditions, all traditionalists ("Throw Pushkin, Dostoyevsky, Tolstoy, etc., overboard from the steamship of modernity"), an end even to language as tradition has conceived it. Khlebnikov is the only Futurist here translated.

Two matters having nothing to do with Russian poetry, but having a great deal to do with this book, need to be at least briefly noted. First, the nature of the editorial selection involved: who has been included, in what quantity, and why, and who has been omitted—and why. And second, what sort of translation is it that the reader of this book can expect to find.

The editorial selection has been aimed at a representative sampling (and I have frequently been guided, I must note, by the excellent editorial work of Mr. Dimitri Obolensky, in his *Penguin Book of Russian Verse*, a book which has been useful to me in a variety of ways). I have tried, also, to give fuller coverage to the more important figures—Pushkin especially, but also Lermontov, Tyutchev, Fet, Blok, Akhmatova. I think the book in fact offers a representative if somewhat eccentric group of translations, showing the growth and development, and hopefully also the excellences, of Russian poetry up to the Revolution. One omission, not I think of any great importance, but vexing to me personally, is the humorous verse of A. K. Tolstoy. I was confident that I could bring it off in English, and thus nicely round out this book. But the first lines of the "Ballad of Steward Larue" emerged like this:

> When the dastard villain knifed him in the chest
> Larue thanked him and smiled.
> When the bloody dagger caught his left side
> he exclaimed "You stab with such zest!"
> The murderer got him from the right, and Larue
> just wagged a finger in his face.
> The assassin filled him with holes like a sieve
> and was asked to tea "at our place."

Which leads to my second question, What sort of translation is here offered the reader? This book is the product of one particular American poet and translator interacting with a group of Russian poets. Some of the translations will reflect, more accurately than others, the essential spirit of their originals. "One thing seems clear: to translate a poem whole is to compose another poem. A whole translation will be faithful to the *matter*, and it will 'approximate the form,' of the original; and it will have a life of its own, which is the voice of the translator. . . . He must make another poem that will speak, or sing, with his own voice" (Jackson Matthews, "Third Thoughts on Translating Poetry," in *On Translation*, p. 67). I will say at once, for example, that I think my Pushkin versions on the whole superior to my Lermontov versions; I am completing a volume of Gumilev translations, but I would have little interest in a book devoted to Zhukovsky, or Derzhavin, or Baratynsky. I am an experienced translator—but also a unitary being. There are advantages to a book and to an approach of this sort, but plainly one of them is not, nor can it be, equivalent reflections of each and all the different poets translated.

The technical aspects of these translations are hard for me to discuss. This is not, I want to stress, an evasion, but a simple fact. I would have liked to set out cogent reasons, for example, as to why I used rhyme in my translations of Blok, but not in my translations of Akhamatova—or why, even less explicably, I could make most of my Pushkin translations rhyme (including *Mozart and Salieri*, which Pushkin did not rhyme!), but not all of them. In general, the twentieth-century poets were harder for me to rhyme, in translation. But I do not know why, though I have some rather vague guesses. Clear answers, if any exist, lie too deep for me to dredge them out: basically, I have done what I have done because it seemed best to me, poem by poem; seemed to work best in English as a representation of what I saw as the poetic quality of the Russian.

Translating poetry may be as subjective an art as writing poetry —it is, for me at any rate—but the reader is entitled to know, also, that these are translations, not imitations. I do not in any way disapprove of translation/imitations—many of the poems in my *From the Vietnamese* are imitations—but I have not in any case tried to compose an original poem, using a Russian poem as a model, as an inspiration, or as a kind of quarry.

A Sprinkling of Russian Proverbs

Pray to God, but do not offend the devil either.

He would tear the skin off a flea.

Love your wife like your soul, and shake her like a pear tree.

We are relatives: we have dried our rags in the same sun.

Where the hostess is beautiful, the wine is good.

A bad peace is better than a good quarrel.

If you are sitting on his cart, you must also sing his song.

He who is destined for the gallows will not be drowned.

They beat you—and do not even allow you to weep.

A fox sleeps, but counts hens in his dreams.

When you die, even your tomb will be comfortable.

Dogs bark, and the wind carries it away.

There will be a holiday in our street, too, some day.

I.

Oral Poetry

"ILYA OF MUROM" is one of the traditional oral heroic songs, or *byliny* ("tales-of-things-that-have-been"), originally sung by court minstrels but more recently sung only by peasant poets. (They are chanted rather than sung, today, where the art still survives, and sometimes there is also a stringed instrument accompanying the recitation. In medieval performance the *gusli*, or harp, was regularly employed.) These songs were not written down until the nineteenth century, when scholars "rediscovered" and recorded them and when the term *byliny* was coined. Textual fidelity to the ancient "original" is therefore impossible to prove; absolute fidelity is inherently very unlikely. The substance and spirit of "Ilya of Murom," however, seems pretty clearly traceable to the eleventh or twelfth centuries. Vladimir Nabokov describes the *byliny* in general as "anonymous remnants of medieval narrative poetry . . . botched by centuries of oral transmission" (*Notes on Prosody*, p. 34). Does this dictum also invalidate the texts of Homer, of Old English poetry, of the Old Testament, and of all work available to us only because of "centuries of oral transmission"?

Ilya of Murom, perhaps the most popular character in the *byliny*, figures in many songs and legends; so too does Prince Vladimir, sometimes described as the King Arthur of Russian folklore. (He seems to represent a combining—and a popularization—of two actual Kievan kings.) Nightingale the Bandit is another well-known folk character, often referred to in later (post-eighteenth-century) Russian writing.

The metric of the *byliny* is a kind of accentual blank verse, though there sometimes is rhyme as well. Much of the spirit of the *byliny* is captured in Lermontov's "A Song about Tsar Ivan Vasilevitch, the Young Bodyguard, and the Valorous Merchant Kalashnikov," composed in 1837 (for a recent translation, see Guy Daniels, *A Lermontov Reader*, pp. 78–98). Soviet poets have frequently imitated the *byliny*. Marc Slonim says of them, perhaps a little too enthusiastically, "The musical rhythm of the *byliny*, the richness of their rhymes and alliterations, the freshness of their metaphors, the majestic pace of their descriptions, and the breadth of their style rank them with the world's greatest epic poetry" (*The Epic of Russian Literature*, pp. 9–10).

"The Lament of Joseph, Son of Jacob," is one of the traditional oral religious poems, or *dukhovnye stikhi*, composed rather later than were the *byliny*. During the period when *byliny* (and their performers) were officially frowned upon, as secular songs tending to corrupt religious feeling, the mendicant pilgrims who had previously sung only *dukhovnye stikhi* began also to sing *byliny*—even on occasion wearing the secular jester garb of *byliny* performers. The *byliny* were thus preserved—and also influenced, certainly, in more religous directions.

Ilya of Murom:
a twelfth-century song

Not a green oak bending,
not paper leaves falling,
but a son on his knees, begging
his father's blessing:
"Oh father, bless me
and let me go to glorious
Kiev, to pray to the holy monks
and miracle-makers,
to bow before Prince Vladimir,
to serve him truly and honorably,
to defend our Christian faith."
    Said old Ivan, a peasant:
"My blessing for good, but not
for evil. Leave Tartars
in peace, when you ride; kill
no Christians where anyone can see."
    Ilya bowed to the ground,
leaped on his horse
and rode across the plain.
His spurs dig at the horse's sides,
through the hide to the black flesh,
and the angry horse
leaps away from the ground,
up over the trees,
just under the clouds.
Its first leap was nine miles,
its second leap sprouted out a well,
and Ilya cut down a green oak
and built a chapel
and carved on the chapel:
A Mighty Hero Rode Here,
Ilya of Murom, Son of Ivan.
The third leap was almost

to Chernigov, where a vast army
stood blocking the roads, three princes
and each with forty thousand men.
Ilya's heart grew excited,
hotter than fire,
hotter than even burning snow.
    And he declared:
"I did not argue with my father,
I wanted to obey my father."
    Then he raised his sabre
and walked through that army,
cutting streets as he turned,
leaving city squares behind him;
he cut through to the three princes.
    And he said, "Oh princes!
Shall I take you prisoner
or cut off your disorderly heads?
If I take you prisoner, there will be roads
for bread to be brought to me,
but if I cut off your heads
I will be cutting a line of kings.
Go home
and let it be known everywhere
that Holy Russia is not a desert,
that there are mighty men in Holy Russia."
    The Governor of Chernigov saw him:
"What a messenger God has sent us!
He has freed us, this man."
    And the Governor said to his noblemen:
"Go, bring that young man
to break bread at my table."
    And the noblemen came to Ilya:
"Oh you great and mighty young man!

6

Tell us your noble name
and your father's name."
"I am Ilya
the son of Ivan."
And the noblemen said to him:
"Oh Ilya of Murom!
Come to our Governor
and break bread at his table."
"I will not come to your Governor,
I do not want to break bread with him.
Tell me which is the straight road
to glorious Kiev."
And the noblemen answered:
"Oh Ilya of Murom!
The straight road is closed,
cut off by the Brown Forest,
by the Smorod river,
and worst of all, by the Birdman Nightingale
the Bandit, sitting as he has sat for thirty years
on twenty-seven oak trees over the road:
no one can pass, on horse or on foot."
Ilya thanked them
and rode into the Brown Forest.
Nightingale heard the horse's hooves
and whistled a mighty blast,
and Ilya's horse stumbled.
And Ilya said to his horse:
"Oh horse, oh hero's horse!
Is this your first time in a dark forest,
Is this the first bird you have heard singing?"
Then Ilya took up his arrows
and shot, and fell short,
and shot, and fell long,

and shot into Nightingale's right eye
and down he tumbled from the twenty-seven oak trees.
Ilya tied him to his saddle
and rode on to glorious Kiev.
  Then Nightingale said:
"Oh Ilya of Murom!
Stop and visit my home."
  And Nightingale's youngest daughter saw them:
"Our father is coming, with a peasant,
blind in one eye, tied to his saddle."
  And Nightingale's oldest daughter came to see:
"Oh infant, idiot! A young man is riding
with our father tied to his saddle."
And they ran at Ilya with clubs.
  And the Birdman Bandit said:
"Be calm, my children,
do not make him angry."
  And Ilya said to Nightingale:
"Why are your children all alike?"
  And Nightingale answered:
"When I have a son, I give him a daughter;
When I have a daughter, I give her to a son,
and my family stays strong."
  Ilya was offended,
and he drew his sabre
and cut them all down.
Then Ilya came to Kiev
and cried in the streets:
"Oh Prince Vladimir, our father!
Are we needed, do you want
mighty men
to bring honor and glory to you
our father, to defend our city

and kill the Tartars?"
      Prince Vladimir answered:
"I need you indeed!
I've hunted for you everywhere.
I offer a horse to each of you,
a Roman horse, a hero's horse."
      And Ilya answered:
"I have my Roman horse, my hero's horse.
This morning I heard Matins with my father,
I rode to hear Mass with you,
but three things delayed me:
An army I defeated at Chernigov;
a bridge I built, nine miles long,
over the river Smorod;
and the time it took me
to shoot down Nightingale the Bandit."
      Father Vladimir, the Prince, said:
"Oh Nightingale the Bandit!
Enter my white stone palace."
      And Nightingale answered:
"I do not serve or obey you,
I serve and obey Ilya of Murom."
      And Vladimir said: "Oh Ilya of Murom!
Order him to enter my white stone palace."
And Ilya ordered him to enter.
      Then Prince Vladimir said:
"Oh you mighty young man,
Ilya son of Ivan!
Order him to whistle a great blast."
      And Ilya answered:
"Oh Father Vladimir, my Prince!
Do not be angry if I lift you
under my arm, and your daughter

under the other."
    And then Ilya said:
"Nightingale, whistle half-strength!"
    And Nightingale whistled full-strength
and the palace roof was blown off
and the iron hinges were broken
and the prince's mighty heroes,
all his noblemen, fell to the ground.
Only Ilya remained standing.
And then he put Prince and Princess on their feet.
    And Prince Vladimir asked:
"Well blown, Nightingale the Bandit!
How could Ilya ever capture you?"
    And Nightingale answered:
"I was dead drunk—
it was my daughter's birthday."
    Ilya did not like his words:
he lifted Nightingale by the head,
carried him to the courtyard,
and threw him up over the trees
and just under the clouds,
and let him fall to the ground,
and threw him up again.
Every bone in Nightingale's body was broken.
And then dinner was served.
    Prince Vladimir said:
"Oh Ilya son of Ivan!
I grant you three places at my table:
one seat at my side,
one seat opposite me,
one seat anywhere you like."
    And then Ilya walked around the table,
and the noblemen and the mighty heroes

were crowded close together,
and Ilya sat opposite the Prince.
    And Aleysha Popovitch, he was angry,
and he drew his knife, and threw it,
and Ilya caught it in the air
and drove it into the table.

The Lament of Joseph, Son of Jacob:
a religious song, fifteenth–seventeenth century

Where shall I call my pain,
who will weep for my name's
sake? You, oh God, only You.
You know my pain,
my Maker, my Creator, only You
oh Giver of all good things.
I would weep, I would sing
for Your mercy, louder and higher,
but where will I find a well of tears?
I would weep both by day and by night,
crying my sins and my fears,
I would weep
like the flowing rivers of Eden
and drown the fires of deep
Hell. Who will give me a speaking
dove? I would send it
to my father Jacob—
oh my father, my father, oh Israel,
oh holy Jacob! Lend
your tears to Joseph your son,
cry to the Lord!
My brothers, your sons
have sold me to an alien land:
my tears have dried like sand,
my tears at leaving you,
and I sit grieving
alone. Oh earth, earth,
who cried to the Lord for the killer of Cain,
lift your voice again
to Jacob, to my father,
to my father Israel!

2.
Before Pushkin

Alexander Petrovitch Sumarokov: 1718–1777

A NOBLEMAN, well educated—and like virtually all the pre-Soviet nobility, deeply influenced by things French—Sumarokov was probably the first Russian gentleman to be a professional writer. He wrote in very many forms, from journalism and literary criticism to lyric songs (as a gentleman he did not publish the latter, but circulated them privately). His comedies and tragedies (he wrote more than twenty plays) led him to the directorship of Russia's first permanent theater (which opened in 1756). His fables began to appear in 1755: they were collected, ultimately, in six volumes.

Not the earliest of Russian fabulists, Sumarokov nevertheless gave the fable its decisive initial impetus. The form became enormously popular in Tsarist Russia; through the use of non-human protagonists, writers could express sharp social criticism without provoking the omnipresent censorship authorities. (One of Sumarokov's most interesting theatrical pieces, the "Chorus to a Topsy-Turvey World," was in its original form refused the censor's permission, and in order to be performed had to be totally rewritten.) Sumarokov is a pioneer, rather than a notable of Russian literature, but as a fabulist and, sometimes, as a lyricist, he can still be read with pleasure.

At the Lion's House:
A Fable

Silence is golden.
Life is delight.
If truth can't be spoken
speech has a price.

Fiesta
at the lion's! All invited!
A noble sight—
but his house was infested,
rich and rank
to the nose.
His gold he banked
with merchants; he chose
to live like his friends—
traders who end
in elaborate filth,
swagger in silk,
not swords.
(To waste few words:
they stink.)
Well, a wolf
sniffed: "I think
your plumbing's gone wrong.
The flavor is strong,
host." The tough
lion roared:
"Shut your face!
Damn it, learn your place!
What kind of
wolf barks at a lion?"
And to teach him the moral
he tore all

his legs off. A terrified ape
cried: "Odor?
Flowers, and incense, and honey and cakes!"
The lion ordered him
grilled as a liar:
"Don't try to
flatter me, beast:
I'm never pleased
by falsehood." And he turned to the fox:
"Your nose is superb,
by God: what kind of herbs
can you sniff?" The box
was tight, but didn't hold:
"Oh, I'b a kohd in my nohd."

Ivan Ivanovitch Khemnitser: 1745–1784

OF GERMAN DESCENT, Khemnitser joined the army at age thirteen, remaining for twelve years and then retiring; his post-army labors involved him in the lexicography of mining and mineralogy. In 1782 he became Russian consul in Smyrna (now Izmir), where he died in 1784.

Khemnitser wrote social satires (unpublished in his lifetime) and a lifetime total of some 104 fables (published only anonymously in his lifetime); the fables were extremely popular for at least half a century after his death. Making use of strong, popular language, keeping the tone light, and avoiding the formal concluding moral, Khemnitser achieved a fairly particularized portrait of the Russian national character. (Significantly, his major literary translation was of La Fontaine.)

Spiders and Flies:
A Fable

A tiny spider thought:
"I've never caught
a really juicy fly—
and I know why.
My net must be wider!"
Small but ambitious, the spider
spun out wide, elated,
and waited.
But all he got
was the same old fleas—not
that no flies
flew by, but their size
and strength tore his snare.
It's true
for people too,
everywhere
you go: luck
goes with weight, not pluck—
the small fly's always the one who gets caught.

Gavrila Romanovitch Derzhavin: 1743–1816

OF A PETTY and very poor noble family, Derzhavin received a modicum of education (learning German, that is, but not French or Latin), then attempted a military career. It took ten years for him to become an officer—but his poetic skill, after about 1780, secured him much more substantial rewards, particularly since some of his best-known work celebrated the Empress Catherine. A cranky, obstinate sort, Derzhavin was unable to stay long in any administrative post (his final post was, briefly, Minister of Justice, in 1802). The last fifteen years of his life were spent quietly and happily on his country estate.

Derzhavin is basically a lyricist. Much of his poetry follows neoclassicist modes; the more interesting part of his work, today, is that which breaks with neoclassicism, becoming individualistic, informal, even eccentric—and often distinctly Romantic. (It has been speculated that his defective formal education may have helped preserve his literary spontaneity though it is worth noting that "The Swan," here translated, is closely modelled on Horace, *Odes*, II, 20.) He is by common consent the best of eighteenth-century Russian poets (Pushkin praised and also imitated him), though the unevenness of his writing is also recognized.

"A Dream Nightingale" was written, as he himself explained, "to prove the mellifluousness of the Russian language"; in the Russian original the letter *r* does not appear. "Time's Unending River" was written three days before Derzhavin's death; it was to be the beginning of a long, philosophical poem called "On Mortality."

A Dream Nightingale

Sleeping on a high hill
I heard you, nightingale,
heard you, lying still
in dreams—your voice now pale,
now distant, now loud,
now weeping, now proud
in my ear; and Callisto's
soft arms and your song
and laughter ran along
my dreams and sweetened my rest.

When sleep turns to death,
drags, and no longer ends,
I'll hear no breath
of this music that sends
sounds of happiness,
of dancing, of girls
singing, of whirling
pride—with so much to miss
I'll savor things here, kiss
my sweetheart, and listen, listen
      to the nightingale.

Country Life

Cities? Why?
Give me the country.
I need no medals
clanking on my chest;
I'm trying to exist
and be happy, liked
and liking.
Tomorrow can strike
as it must: I live today.
Tomorrow you fade away,
everything fades.
Why waste a minute—even one—
when we have so few?
Make boredom pay
for its sins, let sadness be glum!
Money is for fools:
give me peace and my woman.
Where Venus and Bacchus rule
no man
is poor. Healthy
and fed and wined
I'm wealthy—
and while I've time
I'll lie with Milena in the shade.

The Swan

I will leave this fragile earth—
not as men leave,
but like a swan soaring,
and keeping my immortal soul, and singing.

A double image, undying,
sweeping through Peter's Gate,
too exalted for envy,
indifferent, now, to kings and states.

Yes! My father's father was no prince,
but the Muses chose me and blessed me,
and even in Heaven it will be different,
Death himself will take my hand.

No tomb will silence me,
I will never dissolve in the stars, and be dust:
like some magic flute
I will sing with heavenly voices.

Feathers:
down: on my back
white wings:
white radiance soaring

Higher, higher, over
seas, forests, the earth—
and like a hill it lifts
its head, listening as I sing to God.

From Finland to the Ukraine,
from the Turkish sea to the Arctic,
half the world
living as Russians,

All will know me, all in time:
Slavs, Huns, Scythians, Esthonians,
all who flame in Russia's battles,
will lift their hands and exclaim:

"He who flies there tuned his lyre
to his heart's language
and preached peace,
he was happy with everyone's happiness."

No pompous funeral!
No choral songs from the Muses!—
wife: wrap yourself in patience,
don't waste your tears on what looks like a corpse!

Time's Unending River:
a fragment

Time's unending river
floats us along,
kings and countries, strong
and weak, sucked down like feathers.
And anything surviving, an art,
a war of genius,
is plucked and eaten
in the end, crushed like a peasant's cart . . . . . .

Ivan Andreyevitch Krylov: 1769–1844

SON OF A poor army field clerk officer, Krylov was scantily educated and, as quite a small boy, sent to work as a government clerk. At age fourteen he got himself transferred to Saint Petersburg and began to write, turning out a comic opera. Much of his early work was either journalism or satire; none of it was notably successful. In these early years he was something of a progressive radical, and experienced considerable difficulty with Tsarist censorship.

In his twenties and thirties Krylov fumbled about, living pretty much as he could (often as a transient tutor or secretary to titled noblemen), and writing nothing in particular. The satirical journal he founded and edited, *The Spectator*, was suppressed by the government in 1792. This seems, at least for a time, to have driven Krylov away from literature. He had written fables as early as 1788: in 1805 he began to translate La Fontaine—and in 1809 his first collection of fables appeared, to vast acclaim. This first volume was partly translation, partly original work, and after its huge success he wrote only fables, roughly two hundred in his lifetime. Mostly written in the decade 1810 to 1820, they were eventually collected in nine volumes. "In 1812," writes Mirsky, "he received a peaceful and commodious post (practically a sinecure) in the Public Library of St. Petersburg, where he remained for over thirty years . . . . He was noted for laziness, untidiness, good appetite, and shrewed, malicious common sense. His fat, bulky figure was a familiar feature in the drawing-rooms of Petersburg, where he used to sit for whole evenings without opening his mouth, his little eyes half shut or gazing vacantly with an air of boredom and indifference to all around him" (D. S. Mirsky, *A History of Russian Literature*, pp. 69–70).

Krylov is belligerently middle-class in his values. He shows no patience with pretense or with abstractions; with ambitious idealism or with smug stupidity. He is preeminently practical, conservative, and commonsensical.

His epigrams have, in many, many cases, become national proverbs. Although his narrative style sometimes has a faintly musty quality, his dialogue is very racy and alive, drawing heavily on colloquial speech. Still immensely popular, and regularly taught in Soviet schools, Krylov is without question the greatest of Russian fabulists.

A Swan, a Pike, and a Lobster

When friends sing in different keys
nothing comes of it
but trouble.

A swan, and a pike, and a lobster
set up in business
as pullers and haulers.
All three got hitched to a cart
and pulled like devils,
and the load
was right, suitably light,
their muscles were strong—
but their work went wrong:
nothing moved.
Why?
The swan sweated toward the sky,
the lobster hauled sideways,
the pike pulled for the sea.
No one was guilty, no one
worked harder, or better:
all worked well,
but never together.
And the cart's there still,
rotting in our Russian weather.

A peasant with a very stout whip
was driving his geese to market,
and—to be very blunt about it—
the geese were catching it hard.
There was money waiting to be made
and the peasant had drooling visions
of gold (for which dizzying
reason men can be flayed,
too). He had his reasons

all right, but the geese were in pain,
and began to complain
to a perfect stranger: "It's treason!
This fellow beats us
like peasants, treats us
like birds of low feathers,
lumps birds with their betters,
ignores our glorious fathers,
can't read or be bothered
to learn how Rome was saved
by their song, and the respect we're still paid!"

"But what's so special about *you*?"
the stranger asked.
                    "Our fathers—"
                                   "True,
I know, I've read the books.
Your fathers were noble: have you kept their looks?"

"But *they* saved Rome!"

"And *you* have done—
what?"

"What? Well, nothing, yet."

"Then take whatever you get.
Your fathers were noble, were well respected;
when you reach the market, you may be selected
for dinner."

I could dot my P's
and Q's—but the stupid geese
might hiss.

The Wolf and the Shepherds

A wolf, stalking a sheep farm,
crawled to the fence
and saw three shepherds warming
their hearts with the best
ram in the flock, while their dogs
slept and snored.
Cursing to himself, he walked
away: "What a roar
you'd have raised, what a hue and cry,
if instead of shepherds feasting on a sheep,
the well-fed stomach were mine!"

Vasily Andreyevitch Zhukovsky: 1783–1852

BASTARD SON of a Russian nobleman-landowner and a Turkish slave girl, Zhukovsky grew up on his father's estate; he was raised by a pietist stepmother, and in the company of many half sisters and female cousins. He helped educate (and in at least one case fell platonically in love with one of) his cousins; later, he gave Russian lessons to the German fiancée of the future Tsar Nicholas I, and a few years afterward was appointed tutor to Nicholas's heir, the future Tsar Alexander II. As Russia's leading poet, finally, he became the leading teacher and critic of his time, directly befriending many younger writers, including Pushkin, Gogol, and the Ukrainian poet and born serf, Taras Shevchenko (1814–1861). In 1841 he married; his wife was German and very young, and Zhukovsky's final decade was spent in residence in Germany, where he died.

Primarily a translator, Zhukovsky began his career with a rendering of Grey's "Elegy Written in a Country Churchyard"; he produced versions of Goethe, Schiller, Klopstock, Goldsmith, Walter Scott, La Fontaine, *The Odyssey* (though he knew no Greek)—and was instrumental in making Byron known in Russia. He is quoted as saying that "the translators of the poets are the rivals of the poets themselves." He wrote comparatively little original verse, mostly elegies and lyrics, but established himself in a formative position something like that held, in English poetry, by Wordsworth. More personal, and also more autobiographical than previous poets, Zhukovsky brought Romanticism alive in Russia. He was an innovator in formal matters, too, introducing a purer, more melodious diction—and also introducing blank verse, which came to replace the older alexandrine line.

One of the "Songs" ("The Muse Would Come to Me") here translated was written in 1824, by which time Pushkin was very well established, having published his *Ruslan and Ludmilla* some four years earlier. In 1820, to mark that event, Zhukovsky had sent Pushkin a portrait inscribed, "To a victorious pupil from a defeated master." Although Pushkin had written, in 1824—almost thirty years before Zhukovsky's death—"The late Zhukovsky was a good man," by 1825 he reproached others of Zhukovsky's critics with, "Why should we bite the breasts of our common wet-nurse?" And after Pushkin's death, Zhukovsky wrote a bitter letter to Pushkin's "personal" censor, Count Benckendorff: "Which of his works are you acquainted with, except those which the police and a few slandering enemies have called to your attention? He is really a great national poet" (Sidney Monas, *The Third Section*, p. 227).

Song ("The Earth Runs")

The earth runs, runs to the east,
always to the east—
my soul flies
to the east, always to the east:
far in the east,
past the blue forests,
past the blue mountains,
lives my beautiful one.

And here, kept far from her,
I wonder, I wonder over and over
if she is that lovely legend
out of those wonderful old times,
if she came to me only once,
in those ancient times,
if she has left me now
only that happy dream.

Song ("The Muse Would Come to Me")

The Muse would come to me, before,
the young Muse, come down to earth
and bring the wealth
of heaven, and my poems would overflow
as his rays touched
and warmed and quickened life,
and art made much
of life.

The giver of songs
ignores me, now;
my soul longs for
visions, sees nothing; my hands know how
the harp sings, but the strings
are silent—when will it ring
again? Is it still forever, my singing
heart?

But all I have left
from those other times, the dark,
belovèd, bright, forever times, I've kept
in his honor: an Ark
of flowers, some spun,
some real—and I leave them, Spirit
of Beauty, one by one
on your altar here.

You will come when you please,
you will come when you can—
but I know your face, I have seen
your star shining again,
I know its glow,
the magic has not died,
and I know, I know
the past will come to life!

Konstantine Nikolayevitch Batyushkov: 1787–1855

A DIPLOMAT, and on several occasions a soldier in the Napoleonic wars, Batyushkov as a poet broke important new ground. He was passionately fond of the poets of classical Greece (*The Greek Anthology*) and Renaissance Italy (Petrarch, Tasso), and succeeded in bringing much of their clear melodiousness into Russian verse. Often deeply sensual, erotic, sometimes openly pagan, he nevertheless worked toward a sense of balance, of restraint, which could not help but influence the young Pushkin. (John Meresereau, Jr., refers to Batyushkov's "modest sentimentality," in *Baron Delvig's Northern Flowers 1825–1832*, p. 158.) He made his reputation with a light poem, *My Household Gods*, and solidified it with elegies, lyrics, and wryly erotic Greek poems (1817). Batyushkov was also an essayist of talent.

A founder-member of Arzamas (1815), the literary society to which Pushkin was elected in 1817, Batyushkov was neither prolific nor stable. (Reading one of Pushkin's early poems, he is said to have crumpled up the manuscript and thrown it on the floor, swearing, "Oh how this rascal has learned to write!") After 1817 he grew more and more restless and melancholy; a trip to Italy did not help. His poetry turned hauntingly odd—and indeed there are premonitions of instability in much of his work. In 1821 he collapsed: except for brief and passing moments, he was hopelessly insane the rest of his life.

With Zhukovsky, Batyushkov is the great opener-of-doors for the poets who followed him. Derzhavin had made Russian poetry respectable: Zhukovsky and Batyushkov breathed life and grace into it, made it a flexible and joyful instrument.

Pleasure Can Grow

Pleasure can grow in a wild forest,
happiness on the shore of a sea,
harmony sing in the waves' song
on some empty beach.
I love man, but you, oh Nature,
I worship and adore.
Queen of my world, for you memory
is nothing, my cold middle age a bore:
youth and age and past and present
disappear, I can feel once more—
and yet I cannot tell you in words,
and I cannot sit silent at your door.

Hope

Oh spirit, trust in God!
Be brave, be a rock!
Who led me through the flames of war
and brought me out once more?
Whose hand brushed death
away, bent blood-hungry swords,
made bullets drop to the ground?
Who, oh who allowed me to endure
through hunger, and pain, and misfortune,
who kept my soul high
when my feet fell low?
Who took me, from the beginning,
down the secret path of the Good
and stood at my side
when passion flared and burned?

He! He! It was all from Him.
Grace and goodness are from Him,
and love of beauty,
and all clear thoughts.
And from Him, the loveliest of gifts—
a hope of Heaven.
When will I see that still shore,
that land I descended from, once?
When will love burn to peace
in the rivers of the blessed,
and I throw flesh back to dust,
and return, and be born, and eat of His feast?

To My Friends

Here is a complete bibliography
for friendship to lean on.
I hear from a pleasant genius
that my magic craft
lacks a bit of magic, a bit of craft—
but friends can find, anyway, what I felt:
      a history of passions,
        mistakes, errors of mind and heart,
        worries, frivolities, sadness—all dead but here entombed,
        and some gay delight;
        how I used to fall, when I lived, and then get up
        how I died for the world, oh died: yes,
        then sailed along after fortune . . . . . .
And finding a poet's journal
friends can read me
and say:
      "How silly he was, how naïve!
      His tragedies were comic, he never really belonged on
                          Parnassus,
      but he stayed a good friend,
      he never plagued us with his poems
      (and that *is* unusual on Parnassus!)
      and, in short, he lived the way he wrote . . . . . .
      not particularly good; not especially bad."

3.

Pushkin and Friends

Alexander Sergeyevitch Pushkin: 1799–1837

THE GREATEST OF Russian poets, Pushkin was born into an ancient noble family; his mother was the granddaughter of Abraham Gannibal, an Abyssinian brought to Russia and "adopted" by Peter the Great. (Gannibal, or Hannibal—Russian has no *h* sound —rose to be Peter's engineer general, and died less than twenty years before Pushkin's birth.) Pushkin was educated at home, in a deeply French and rather superficially cosmopolitan atmosphere. His father's library was an excellent one—in French, of course. Russian was not spoken in the house; Pushkin's maternal grandmother was the only member of his family with whom he spoke Russian. Pushkin seems to have read widely in French literature; Voltaire was his first major literary model. It is said that when he entered the *lycée*, in 1811, Pushkin had some difficulty in writing Russian; by his own admission he remained rather more at ease in French, even in his later years.

Pushkin's literary talents were clear from a very early age. His uncle, Vasily Lvovitch Pushkin (1767–1830), was a prominent minor poet; such figures as Nikolai Mikhailovitch Karamzin (1766–1826), the immensely influential literary and linguistic reformer, and the poet Vasily Zhukovsky, were intimates of the household—and these older writers not only were aware of Pushkin's talents, but openly recognized them. Before he had graduated from the *lycée*, in 1817, Pushkin was admitted to membership in their lighthearted but serious and influential literary club, Arzamas. Many of Pushkin's *lycée* classmates and many others among his friends were Decembrists—a revolutionary movement whose coup was badly botched in December 1825, and whose participants were ruthlessly punished—and the general tone of his personal circle was progressive, even radical, and also rather dissolute. From 1817 to 1820, Pushkin's life was full of high talk, hard drinking, gambling, whoring—and high society, too. And hard work: in March 1820, he completed his first long poem, the 3,000-line *Ruslan and Ludmilla*. But in May, a month before actual publication, the Tsar ordered Pushkin exiled to South Russia; assorted anti-Imperial epigrams, an ode praising tyrannicide, and some public gestures in support of political violence were the cumulative causes.

Pushkin remained in exile for six years. For the first four years he visited strange southern places, probably lived for some days with a tribe of gypsies, sought eagerly what cultivated company he could find, lived rather widly—and wrote a very great deal, including most of *The Gypsies*, the first of his mature narratives, and the early portions of *Evgeny Onegin*. In a letter dated 4 November 1823, announcing the beginning of this "novel in verse," he declared: "There's no use even to think of publishing; I am writing the way I feel like writing. Our censorship is so arbitrary that it is impossible to determine the sphere of one's activity with it. It is better not even to think of it. . . ." (*The Letters of Alexander Pushkin*, p. 141). In 1824 Pushkin was reexiled, confined to his family's estate and ordered not to leave it: a letter of his, in praise of atheism, had been opened and read by the postal authorities, and this provided the official rationale for his new punishment. In fact, the cause was ugly personal intrigue and hatreds, in part set in motion by one of his own friends. He read most of the time; listened a good deal to his old nurse's recitations of Russian folktales (*Le Coq d'Or*, here translated, stems directly from this source); wrote *Boris Goudonov*, many, many lyrics (including "The Prophet" here translated), finished *The Gypsies* and three chapters of *Evgeny Onegin*—and wrote frantically to Zhukovsky, well placed at court to be of use to him, to help free him from exile.

In 1826 Pushkin was permitted to return to Moscow, his birthplace, and in 1827 to Saint Petersburg—but not without conditions. He was placed under the Tsar's personal supervision. The general censorship therefore did not apply to him, but he could publish nothing without the Tsar's express approval. The actual supervision was exercised by Count Alexander Benckendorff (1783–1844), chief of the Third Section of the Private Chancery (which in turn controlled the Russian Secret Service)—and Pushkin's life was closely watched, though he did not know it, by Third Section agents. Indeed, as Sidney Monas points out, "Not only Pushkin but all his relatives were watched" (*The Third Section*, p. 205). Many of Pushkin's closest friends were already in exile (or dead), as Decembrists: it is fairly clear that the Tsar consciously intended his "liberality" to the poet to mitigate the effect of harsh suppression of that coup. "There is no doubt," says Mirsky, "that Pushkin, had he had the opportunity, would have joined the rebels and shared their fate; when in September (1826) Nicholas asked him where he would have been on 15th December, he answered without hesitation: 'On the Senate Square with the rebels'" (D. S. Mirsky, *Pushkin*, p. 93). The "personal" supervision and censorship were very real: "The Third Section's agents followed Pushkin, searched the papers of his friends, opened his mail" (*The Third Section*, p. 209). *Boris Goudonov* could not be published until 1831; Benckendorff rebuked Pushkin on hearing that the poet had read this long poem to some friends before submitting it to the Tsar. And *The Bronze Horseman*, which Pushkin refused to revise to order, was not published in his lifetime.

The nagging realities of Pushkin's life, from 1826 to his death in 1837, are perhaps difficult for us to appreciate. The Tsar's grip on him was never relaxed; in 1831 he made a disastrously bad marriage, his wife being frivolous, vain, and flirtatious; Russian high society, corrupt and often vicious, nagged and gnawed at him—"Pushkin-baiting seems to have become something of a sport in the gilded circles," says Monas (ibid., p. 215)—and by 1837 he was prepared to do almost anything to escape, to retire back into the country. That permission had been repeatedly denied—in part, it seems probable, because the Tsar enjoyed flirting with Pushkin's very beautiful wife. Indeed, to better enjoy her company, the Tsar had given Pushkin a humiliating court appointment (humiliating because usually reserved for much younger men), which compelled him to attend court functions. His wife's flirtation with Baron George d'Anthès, a foreign officer (and something of a favorite of Count Benckendorff), was rather more serious, and d'Anthès's marriage to Madame Pushkin's younger sister did not improve matters. Pushkin was receiving vicious anonymous letters (one invited him to membership in the Most Serene Order of Cuckolds), he was increasingly desperate, and, acting with great care and secrecy (to avoid friendly interference), he challenged d'Anthès to a duel. Almost certainly, he did not expect to be killed, he expected only to be exiled in punishment for the offense of duelling—but d'Anthès's bullet hit him in the abdomen and he died two days later. (Wounded, Pushkin first said, "Je suis blessé," and then, lying on the ground, he motioned his seconds away, saying, again in French: "Je me sens assez de force pour donner mon coup." He held himself up on one arm, fired, cried "Bravo!" and threw up his pistol when d'Anthès fell also—but d'Anthès was not seriously hurt. An attempt at reconciliation was firmly rebuffed: "Au reste, c'est égal," said Pushkin. "Si nous rétablissons tous deux, ce sera à recommencer" [Mirsky, *Pushkin*, p. 222].)

I cannot hope to sum up Pushkin's poetic achievement. His range was immense, his fecundity staggering. Russian literature was in its infancy when Pushkin began his career: he left it fully matured. Forty years after his death Dostoyevsky wrote, "Everything we have comes from Pushkin" (Alexander Pushkin, *Pushkin*, trans. John Fennell, p. xxiv)—and it has been said that *Evgeny Onegin* was the egg from which all of Turgenev's plots were hatched. Pushkin could handle every kind of diction, from the loftiest to the lowest—and often all in the same poem (see especially *The Bronze Horseman*, here translated). He was able to assimilate, to absorb and make totally his own, influences of the most diverse sort, and from a wide variety of literature and cultures. His private library contained 4,000 books, in many languages and on many subjects. He learned English in order to read Byron, but the influence was transcended in Pushkin's own work, most notably in that most Byronesque of his poems, *Evgeny Onegin*. (The best translation, to date, is that by Walter Arndt.) "Evgeny Onegin is the opposite of [Byron's] *Don Juan*," notes Edmund Wilson, "in being a work of unwavering concentration. . . . Artistically, he has outstripped his time; and neither Tennyson in *In Memoriam* nor Baudelaire in *Les Fleurs du Mal* was ever to surpass Pushkin in making poetry of classical precision and firmness out of a world realistically observed" ("In Honour of Pushkin," *The Triple Thinkers*, pp. 43–44). His prose, too, was brilliant: J. Thomas Shaw speaks neatly of Pushkin's "naked, saturated [prose] style" (*The Letters of Alexander Pushkin*, p. 43), and Marc Slonim notes that, in addition, "Pushkin had an astounding gift of spontaneous versification and he often enlivened informal gatherings with his dazzling improvisations" (*The Epic of Russian Literature*, p. 97).

Turgenev has a brief pen portrait of Pushkin, as seen at a concert, a very few days before his death: "He was standing at the door, leaning against the lintel and, his hands crossed on his broad chest, looking round with a dissatisfied air. I remember his small, dark face, his African lips, the gleam of his large white teeth, his pendent side-whiskers, his dark, jaundiced eyes beneath a high forehead, almost without eyebrows, and his curly hair" (*Turgenev's Literary Reminiscences*, pp. 107–108).

Volumes of Pushkin's poetry, his shorter fiction, and his letters, as translated by Alla Burago and myself, are in progress. The first of them should appear in 1972.

Grapes

Spring goes, roses
fade: how quick, how fine,
but then I love vines
under the hill, ripe
with grapes in bunches—
the shine of my black ground,
the glow, the delight of autumn,
thin and gold and clear
like a young girl's hands.

The Prophet

Spiritual dryness dragged me
through a desert,
and where roads crossed a six-winged seraph
came,
touching my eyes, light
like a dream,
and like a frightened eagle
I saw everything—
touching my ears
till they rang with bellowing,
and I heard the sky shudder
and angels' wings up high,
and animals under the waters,
and vines as they grew—
and bending to my mouth
he ripped out my tongue, emptily
wagging, deceitful,
and his right hand dripped blood
as he fitted a serpent's
wise forked tongue to my lips—
and splitting my chest with a sword
he pulled out my heart
and gave me a burning coal.
I lay in the desert
like a corpse.
And then the Voice of God:
"Up, oh prophet, go see and hear,
and filled with My will
cross land and ocean
and ignite men's hearts with your Word!"

Love Song

Holding your slender body,
passionately praising love
and you, tender, warm,
you rise, oh my dear,
with a knowing smile,
silently withdraw
from my arms,
mistrustful,
remembering others who were false
as they swore faith;
you listen sadly,
hardly listen, scarcely hear . . . . . .
and I curse my own sly
beginnings, and the hours
in silent dark
gardens,
waiting—I curse whispered love-words,
mysterious love-rhymes,
the kisses of swooning girls,
and their tears, and their sighs.

The Cossack

In midnight mist
and blackness
a Cossack
rode along the river,

Hat to the side,
fur coat filthy,
pistols at his knees,
sabre gliding

To the grass. His horse
walked free, walked slow,
long mane flowing,
walked him along

Past huts, falling
fences, a road
to a village, a road
to forests.

"No girls in trees,"
he thought.
"All uncaught
birds are caged for the night."

But he pulled the reins,
shoved with a spur,
and the horse strained
and pounded earth

To the village. A moon-
silvered sky.
An uncaught bird high
and sad at her room

Window: seen! Ah, seen!
And softly steers,
and quiet veers
there where she thinks unseen.

"In midnight mist
and blackness
even a Cossack's
horse stumbles. Please:

Water, sweet." "Oh,
in midnight mist and blackness
I'm afraid to go
to a Cossack's

Horse." "Ah no,
be kind."
"I'm afraid. No."
"Ah, trust me, find

Your gold time here,
forget fear,
where I am is love:
come. Come. Come.

We will ride together
and far, wherever
you ride will be heaven
with me, forever."

And then? She came,
shy but willing,
murmured her name,
thrilled,

And they galloped away
and lived in heaven
for fourteen days.
Then he found someone better.

Autumn: a fragment

Is there anything my sleepy head
doesn't think of?
                              DERZHAVIN

(1)
October: leaves shake,
fall, branches wave black.
Winds blow cold, ice breaks
in the corners of the road but cracks
across the pond; the river still runs;
my hunting neighbor attacks
with dogs and guns,
and deer and wheat go under;
hounds in the woods bay like thunder.

(2)
This is my season—not slopping
dripping spring, damp
and warm in the heart, implanting
desire. Nothing's flopping
in winter, smooth and cold
where the sled slides, and the moon
burns, when hot in her fur she pants
and, shaking, reaches for your hand.

(3)
And steel runners hiss
on river glass.
And peasants drink. And dance . . . . . .
But snow for half a year bores
even the bears: who can roar
in the wind forever, kiss
Armida under her furs—or glumly
sit and stare at a hot stove-sun?

(4)
Ah summer! Colder, cleaner,
bugless, I could stand you—
but you roast our brains, steam us
like meadows, and bland
as puddles we dream of water—
blessing Old Mother Winter. Having hailed her
for leaving, we toast her
in the heat with ices in frosted pails.

(5)
No one knows autumn;
I love it for its gentle glow
and quiet face, caught in
beauty like an unloved child lonely
and unknown. Only Fall
for me: half perfect is enough,
a quarter perfect; all
I want is this elegant roughness.

(6)
A reason? My eyes see her
like a tubercular girl dying
with a smile,
happy to greet
another morning—no scolding,
no tears; death too grows older.
Today she's alive, her cheeks burn red.
Today is today. Tomorrow she's dead.

(7)

Oh sad-eyed season, enchanting!
Your fading beauty is my delight:
trees in gold and purple, the bite
of wind whirling in the leaves, a scant
sun, skies
rolled with mist, then frost,
then signs
of snow and hail in the north.

(8)

In the autumn I flower:
cold air is my tonic, I relish
my days, each hour by hour;
I sleep at night, I eat
by the clock; my heart is free
and wanders. And I tell such
truths of myself as science has proved.
(Science in poetry? My metaphors move!)

(9)

My horse trots up, I mount,
he throws his mane and his rider
crosses hard fields, counts
frozen valleys echoing hooves, hears sliding
ice flaws. The sun
burns fast, my fire
flares brighter, I stare, or read,
or let my log-dazed mind go to seed.

(10)
And there is no world, and my fancy
rules in the silence, and poetry
leaks from my soul, and my heart
shakes, and I echo, and art
like a dream bursts
from my lips and guests
crowd through the air, thirsting
for my word, my hand, begging for their parts.

(11)
And my brain boils up rhymes
and words begin to run
and my fingers find
a pen, a paper—here—a poem's begun.
Like a ship in a calm
when sailors suddenly leap
at the masts and the canvas is on
and filling, and she slides and creeps.

(12)
And sails! And where shall we sail to? . . .

A Winter Morning

Sun and frost: a lovely day.
You're still asleep, my sweet:
my beautiful, awake!
Open eyes heavily sealed,
there's dawn
breaking in the north.

It blew, last night,
the sky was black,
the pale moon's light
was yellow, when clouds cracked,
and you sat
sadly—but today: see!

Skies all blue
and snow shining
in the sun—this tiny
forest still dark, frost
green on the fir,
rivers sparkling in ice.

We've an amber room
and a crackling
hot stove:
I love our sofa—
but why not go tracking
our mare and the sleigh?

It's smooth on morning snow,
my sweet, throwing
the horse her reins!
And we'll see bare fields
and winter woods
and the lakes I love . . . . . .

Count Vorontsov

Half noble, half grocer,
half learnèd, half fool,
half crook—but don't give up hope of
seeing him whole.

Jealousy: a fragment

No more wind and rain, but clouds
hang black and heavy as lead;
the moon slides up from the trees
misty as a ghost.
It all hangs on my heart.
Somewhere, the moon is bright,
the night air warm,
the sea holds across the horizon
like a soft full sheet.
And it's time: she climbs down
to the shore and the waves,
sits sad, alone.
Alone . . . . . . no one weeps for her, begs for her,
blindly kissing her knees.
Alone . . . . . . no one's mouth opens
on her shoulders, her wet lips, her white, white breasts.

.   .   .   .

.   .   .   .

.   .   .   .

Her love is worth more than any of them:
No? But you're alone . . . . . . and you're crying . . . . . .
                              . . . . . . I'm pleased.

.   .   .   .

Yet if . . . . . .

I'm Here, Ensilda

I'm here, Ensilda,
here at your window.
Seville is all sleeping
and dark.

For loving or fighting,
with my sword and my lute,
I'm here in my cloak,
at your window.

Can you still be sleeping?
Listen to my lute!
If the old man hears too
I'll kill him.

Hang silk from your window,
Hurry, Ensilda!
You're slow—are you still
alone?

I'm here, Ensilda,
here at your window.
Seville is all sleeping
And dark.

The Water Nymph

High over a lake, in a forest,
a monk sought Heaven,
afflicting his senses
with labor, with prayer, with deprivation.
His wooden spade
dug slowly at his grave,
and his prayers to the saints
begged an old man's death.

One summer, bent
in front of his hut, he sent
prayers to his God.
Then the forest went black,
mist steamed on the lake,
and a cloud-covered moon, bright red,
rolled in the sky.
He watched,

Stared, afraid,
not understanding the lake
or himself . . . . . . It boiled,
then suddenly grew calm again . . . . . .
And pale as a night
shadow, white
as early snow, a naked
woman climbed up, silent, and sat

Watching the old monk, and slowly
combing her long
wet hair. He shook
and looked, and looked.

She waved to him, waved,
nodded . . . . . . then like a fading
star suddenly dived
back in the still lake.

He could not sleep,
that night; he could not pray,
next day.
He saw her in front of him, always
the same.
And that night she came
again, beautiful, naked, pale,
above the still lake.

She watched him coming, smiled,
blew kisses,
splashed in the water, played like
a child, cried, moaned,
"Oh monk, monk, come,
come to me, come to me!"
Then she sank in the clear
water; he could hear

Nothing. The third day he sat breathless
by the lake, waiting.
Darkness covered the forest,
and he waited . . . . . .
At dawn
he was gone;
only, some boys saw
his beard, later, swimming in the lake.

The Nightingale and the Rose

Spring in a silent garden, and dark,
as a nightingale sings to a rose.
The rose neither listens nor feels,
asleep as the bird sings its heart.
But how different for men?
Poet, can you ever succeed?
Cold beauty can't hear, won't feel,
just blooms, lovely, forever immune to your song.

You Live Somewhere Else

You live somewhere else, not here;
It's far. You sailed.
I cried painful tears,
time seemed impaled
on sadness. My hands
held you, kept you, a moment,
my moans
begged you to prolong the agony. Your plan

Pulled lips
apart, broke a bitter kiss.
From the end of exile
you called me to join you. "Next time,"
you said, "I'll smile
from under a deep blue sky,
from under dark olive branches,
and we'll kiss." But no chance

Was left: blue
is the sky, dark
are the olives, and you
are asleep forever, marked
with nothingness—pain
and beauty in the grave.
But that kiss: it's a debt
you owe me. I'll collect it yet.

I Loved You

I loved you—I love you, still,
too much—but forget
this love that pressed
sadly against your will.

I loved you in silence, without
hope, but true, jealous, afraid.
I pray
that someone may love you again, the same way.

Mozart and Salieri (1830)

*Antonio Salieri (1750–1825), in his time a noted operatic composer
and also a conductor, was one of Mozart's chief contemporary rivals.
It was said that, at the premiere of* Don Giovanni, *Salieri hissed,
rose from his seat, and left the theater; gossip also had it that Salieri
had poisoned Mozart. Pushkin's comment on these apochryphal
stories was that anyone who could hiss* Don Giovanni *was certainly
capable of poisoning its composer.*

Rimsky-Korsakoff used Pushkin's play as the text for an opera.

*Pushkin's Russian does not rhyme; in a fairly free way, this transla-
tion does rhyme. I have tried, through rhyme, to come closer to what
Pushkin's tone might be, in today's English. But I am very aware that
readers who know this play in Russian may feel the attempt unjustifiable.*

Mozart and Salieri

Scene i. A room

Salieri:
They say: no justice on earth.
But there's none in Heaven, by God!
It's as clear as a simple scale. My birth
gave me art and my love
for art. In our old church,
as a child, when the organ rang
I wept, sweet and uncontrolled,
and I stood as long as it played.
As a boy I renounced amusement:
everything not music I pushed away,
gave myself, swore myself, then
and since, to music alone.
Music! It was dull, at first,
and hard. I failed, my bones

cracked with effort. I made craft
a god, bent melody in half,
took only the proper paths,
faithful, observant, my fingers
finally agile, my ear becoming ripe.
I sliced up sound, made strings
of harmony by formula, dissected windpipes.
When science was mastered, I'd begin
to create, to imagine—
but quietly, afraid of fame.
Sometimes I'd slave for days,
weeping and laughing,
then coldly burn my heap
of ideas and passion, my shaft
of broken inspiration. No, no: when Gluck revealed
an unknown world, treasures dark
and new, I threw knowledge
aside, learning I'd loved and trusted,
and into that stark
new world I pursued him, with courage,
I lusted
only after truth,
uncomplaining—running like a man lost
and hunting news
from anyone he meets. It cost
me years of sweat: I won,
the art was mine, fame was mine,
men listened with their hearts, they loved what I'd spun.
I smiled, peaceful, at these signs
of success, at anyone's success, nakedly
happy, hard at work, and glad
for all good music and its makers.

Envy? Never! Bad
Parisian ears cheered Piccini; I heard
Gluck and was dizzy.
But envy? Not a word
of serpent poison; I never lay impotently
gnawing dust
with toothless gums:
not proud Salieri! No one,
no one, could have called me jealous. And now I must
admit—now—here, alone—
that envy's so deep in my bones
that I ache, I burn,
when suddenly Heaven throws
its sacred gift, free,
immortal, not to me
who yearned
and sweated, begged and slaved,
but casts genius to a puppy,
a buffoon. How I craved
that gift. Ah, Mozart, Mozart!

[*Enter Mozart*]
Mozart:

                                    Eh,

You saw me coming!
I've a joke for you, Salieri; it's stunning!

Salieri:
You've just come in?

Mozart:
Yes. I had some pieces,
new ones, to bring you, and near the inn—
oh, Salieri, it's a treat!—

I heard a violin!
Oh, it's rare, it's rare:
a blind fiddler, grinding out
"*voi che sapete*!" What a find!
I stared, I stood and stared,
Salieri, and then I brought him here.

[*Enter blind fiddler*]
My friend, a bit of Mozart, please!
[*The fiddler plays* "voi che sapete" *and Mozart roars with laughter*]

Salieri:
This doesn't offend your ear?

Mozart:
Incredible, Salieri! You're teasing!

Salieri:
No. I see nothing funny
in a vulgar painter mocking Titian,
or a shallow wit
disfiguring Dante—for money
or laughter. Leave us, fiddler!

Mozart:

       Wait.

Here, drink my health.
[*Exit old fiddler*]

     You're in a state,
Salieri. I'll come
some other time.

Salieri:

      What did you bring?

Mozart:
Some casual things.
I couldn't sleep, last night;
I thought of a few ideas. Today
I scribbled them out. I'd play them,
Salieri, to see what you think,
but I see you've no time.

Salieri:
                What a frightful
notion! No time for you? Always,
Mozart, always. Sit down. Play.

[*Mozart goes to the piano*]

Mozart:
Imagine—anyone—me, perhaps,
but younger. In love—not much, just a little.
Sitting with a girl, or a friend, cracking
jokes—with you, Salieri. Then a brittle
sense of darkness, a sudden vision
of the grave—that sort of stuff. Well, here: listen.

[*He plays*]

Salieri:
Carrying this you could stop
at an inn and watch
a fiddler? My God, Mozart: you're too good
for yourself!

Mozart:
              And the music is good?
Salieri:
Ah: passion, strength—and harmony!
You're a god, Mozart. Yes, you'd deny it,
but you are.

Mozart:
                    Not me! Really? It could be......
but my deity needs food.

Salieri:
Excellent. Dine with me.

Mozart:
Yes. I'd like that, Salieri. Fine.
Just let me go home, warn my wife.
I'll come back.

[*Exit Mozart*]

Salieri:
                    I'll wait. Don't forget.
No! This is fate, fate. I yield,
I see my mission: to shield us,
now, before it's too late, before
all music's priests and servants are ruined—
not Salieri but all! How much more
can he do, living? He's strewn
a few wonders: will he climb
higher? Will he lift us
to Heaven, or leave us where we were—sickened
without him? The time
is now: he sings like an angel, surely;
his songs are from Heaven. But we're ruled
by dust, we're men, not gods. He'll quicken
desire, then fly off. Fly, then, the quicker
the better!
                    This drug's a gift
from Isora. I carry it
always, waiting—and when life's led me
to pure pain, or I've broken bread

with someone I hate, someone unwary,
I've wondered—and held back,
not afraid, not hating for no reason,
not thinking death black,
but only that the season
seemed wrong. "Why die?"
I thought. "I may find
new heights,
new music, nights
of inspiration. A new Haydn
could create
and I enjoy."
Or with those I hate: "Wait:
time may bring worse,
some curse
of fate may soil
existence—and this drug is the cure!"
It is, it is: a new Haydn and pure
hate together—and I know
your use. Oh precious gift
of love, you'll glow,
tonight, in friendship's
cup. Tonight! So.

Scene ii. Mozart and Salieri, at dinner.
A private room in an inn

Salieri:
You're sad.

Mozart:
            What? Salieri, you're mad!

Salieri:
Mozart, you're worried, I see it.
We've eaten well, the wine
was superb, but you're silent.

Mozart:
It's true. My *Requiem*'s on my mind.

Salieri:
A *Requiem?* You've been working long?

Mozart:
Three weeks, yes. But there's something wrong:
I didn't tell you?

Salieri:
                 No.

Mozart:
                Then listen.
One day I was late. Someone
had called. All night I whispered
to myself: "Who could have come,
who? And for what?"
He came again; I was out.
He came the third time, I was playing with my son,
I was called.
He was all
in black, he commissioned a *Requiem*, then bowed
and left. Courteous, brief.
And at once I sat myself down
and wrote. And he hasn't come again—
which is good, I'd be grieved
to give my *Requiem* away,
It's ready, and all, but then . . . . . .
well, in the meantime . . . . . .

Salieri:

What?

Mozart:

It's hard to say . . . . . .

Salieri:
Say what?

Mozart:

That man in black: day
and night I see him,
he hunts me like a shadow. Everywhere.
Right now I almost see him,
here, right here.

Salieri:
Stop! You're being a child!
Be sensible. Old Beaumarchais,
he'd always say:
"Salieri, when your brain goes wild
and black, break open champagne—
or read my *Figaro* again!"

Mozart:
Right! He was your friend, of course;
you wrote *Tarare* for him, lovely
stuff. One tune soars
in my skull when I'm gay . . . . . . dee-tov, dee-tov . . . . . .
Salieri: is it true
that Beaumarchais poisoned a fellow?

Salieri:
It seems unlikely. He was far too witty
for such things.

Mozart:
                    A genius, too,
like you and me. Genius and crime are pretty
different—no?

Salieri:
You think so?

[*Slips the poison into Mozart's glass*]

                    A toast!

Mozart:
To your health, to the tie
between Mozart and Salieri,
both sons of harmony.

[*Mozart drinks*]

Salieri:
Wait, don't toast alone! Without me—why?

[*Mozart throws his napkin on the table*]

Mozart:
Enough.

[*Goes to the piano*]

                    Now, Salieri, my *Requiem*.

[*Plays*]

                              Are you crying?

Salieri:
A new kind of tears. I feel
pain and pleasure together; it's like
the end of some horrible job, a healing
knife
cutting a dead limb! Go on—these tears—
go on, my soul will overflow.

Mozart
If only the world could know
such feelings! But no, if men were to hear
as you hear, Salieri, there'd be
no world: who'd choose needy
work? We'd all be free—
and artists. Meanwhile,
in this world as it is, we're only a few,
we priests of beauty. That's true,
No?—But I'm ill, today, I'll go home
and sleep. I'll be better. Goodbye!

[*Exit Mozart*]

Salieri:
Till we meet again.
                         I'm alone—
You'll sleep forever, Mozart! But I,
am I less than a genius? "Crime
and genius are different"—he says.
No. Consider Michael Angelo—
that story must be true.
He built the Vatican, and he murdered too.
No?

Le Coq d'Or (1831–1832)

This was one of a set of three skazki, *or fantastic folktales, written according to tales told Pushkin by his nurse, Arina Rodionovna. The other two are* The Tsar Saltan *and* The Dead Princess and the Seven Champions, *the former generally considered one of his masterpieces, the latter not placed on the same level.* Le Coq d'Or (*or* The Golden Cockerel: *I prefer the French title made famous by Rimsky-Korsakoff's musical setting) is rather less fairy-talelike than the other two; it has more irony, it is less faithful to the unadulterated folktale tradition from which it comes.*

Le Coq d'Or

In the kingdom of triple-nine,
in the world of triple-ten,
Tsar Dadon ruled. From the time
of his youth he'd loved war, and again
and again bullied his neighbors.
But now he was old, and age
led him to an interest in peace:
war would rest—like the Tsar.
But countries near and far
felt his weakness,
sent armies from every direction,
first east, then west: inspection
in the south—but trouble from the north.
His generals whirled, and fought,
ran to the mountains, the coast,
always marching too late.
Tsar Dadon wept with rage,

lay miserably awake at night:
his army was huge, and his land,
but nothing went right,
his life was torture, his grand
empire crumbled at the edge,
always needed repair.
In despair
he sent to a eunuch
who'd solved stars and knew men,
who was old and wise;
his servants begged
for magic and advice.

    The holy man came, bowed
to the Tsar, and drew a gold
cock from his bag. "You've found
a true watchman, bold
and honest. Mount him on a steeple.
If your empire is peaceful
he'll sleep—but if war begins,
if invaders come,
if anything evil is done
anywhere you rule, in an instant
he'll wake,
spread his feathers, shake
his comb, and crow,
and turn his face
to your trouble."
The Tsar promised double
rewards, triple, whatever
he asked:
"I'll never
forget this," and he laughed

with delight. "Your very first wish
is granted
as though it were mine."
     They planted
the golden cock high
on a steeple. Wherever danger is,
the cock knows it,
wakes,
shakes
his feathers and crows,
"Kiri-ku-ku"—
and the Tsar always knew
in time, and his neighbors learned
he was ready, and grew calm and afraid.

And a year turned
into two,
then three, full of peaceful days.
Then suddenly the cock awoke
and the people screamed and the Tsar
was summoned: "Father
of the people, come!" "Who's broken
what law?" Tsar Dadon yawned,
"What's up?" "Disaster!" they cried.
"What? Where's disaster?" he sighed,
"What's wrong?"
"The cock!" his general explained,
"He's crowing again,
and the people are crying with fear."
The Tsar could hear,
could see the golden feathers shaking
in the sun,

and facing east.
"Send my oldest son at once,
with an army. Whoever's breaking
the peace must be dealt with. Be fast,
soldiers, up on your horses."
They marched, and the golden bird
and Tsar Dadon slept.

     Eight days and no word:
is it war? Have they fought?
Tsar Dadon could get
no news—then the cock crowed
and another army ran
to the east, the younger son told
to rescue his brother.
And the bird's clamor
was still. But no word from one or the other!
Another
eight days, and the people in fear—
and the cock crows!
And the Tsar knows
there's nothing else, old heroes
must help if they can, so he marches himself.

They rush through day and night,
the solders complaining, frightened
by silence, missing the sight
of a camp or the signs
of a battle: no wounded, no dead,
nothing. "What dreadful
thing . . . . . . ?" thinks the Tsar.
Eight days go by: just in time
they see a silken tent, not far,

in the mountains; they climb;
silence—
but down a steep ravine both armies lie,
destroyed.
Tsar Dadon hurries to the tent . . . . . .
sees spread on the bloody soil
his sons, dead,
lying without armor, heads
bare, stabbed,
one by the other.
On the red-stained, trampled grass
their horses wander . . . . . .
"My children, my children!" the Tsar howls,
"My eagles, both trapped!
This hour
is my death too,
I shall die with you!"
His soldiers shriek, the valleys groan,
the mountain quivers to its heart—
and suddenly the tent opens . . . . . .
and a woman, young, the queen of Shamakar,
glowing like dawn,
steps softly through.
And the Tsar is stunned,
still, like a bird of darkness
in the light, and he forgets his sons
in her eyes.
And she smiles
and bows
and clasps
his hand
and

takes him in her tent.
Cowed,
dazed, he lets her lead him
to table, send him
to her brocaded bed,
feed him
and please him as she likes.
And for the days of a week,
bewitched, he feasts in her arms.

At last, with his army
and the queen
he starts
for his home.
Rumor has been
before him, his people roam
the streets in confusion. When his chariot is seen
at the gates, they roar
and chase at the wheels,
hailing Tsar and queen.
And Dadon greets them, like the hero of a war . . . . . .
and sees, suddenly, in a peakèd hat
white as his hair, white
as a swan, the eunuch whose cock sat
in peace on the city's heights.
"Greetings, my wise man!
Come closer, if you want. Speak.
Have you something to ask?"
"O Tsar," says the eunuch,
"I've come, at last,
to settle accounts. You swore—
remember?—to reward me

like a friend, to grant
my very first wish as your own.
Then give me this woman,
Shamakar's queen."
The Tsar only stared.
"What? You're a madman!
You seem
sane, but the devil's in your beard.
I swore,
of course,
but what's a woman to you?
Who's the Tsar? Enough!
I'll give you a horse
from my stables, make you a duke,
give you my gold,
half the country to rule—
ask, and they're yours."
The old
eunuch answered: "Only
the woman, Shamakar's queen!"
The Tsar spat at his feet.
"No!
To hell with you!
Now you'll have nothing:
go,
before it's too late. Drag him away!"
The old eunuch stayed,
tried to dispute,
but with some people words are dangerous:
the Tsar struck him in the head
with his mace; he fell, and was dead.
Everyone shook—but it suited

the queen to cry "Hee, hee," and "Ha, ha."
Evil was nothing to her.
The Tsar, trembling, disturbed,
somehow gave her
a smile, and rode into town . . . . . .
and then a sound
of bells lightly ringing
and the gold bird
fluttered down,
straight to the Tsar's chariot.
It perched on his head,
spread
its feathers, pecked at his skull,
and flew up, up . . . . . .
and Dadon fell to the ground,
groaned just once,
and was dead.
The queen? Gone, in a flash.
Don't ask
my sources: the story's not true,
but you can find things in it, all of you!

The Bronze Horseman (1833)

The poem originated in Pushkin's desire, beginning in 1831, to continue Evgeny Onegin: *the identity of the two heroes' names is not accidental (although* Evgeny *provides a Russian poet with luxuriant rhyming possibilities).* Pushkin eventually settled on the very different subject of The Bronze Horseman—*and at that point wrote the poem very rapidly. His foreword explains that "the incident described in this tale is based on fact. The details are taken from contemporary magazines. The curious may verify them from the material compiled by V. I. Berkh." The actual flood had taken place in 1824; Pushkin had contributed, anonymously, to its victims.*

Written in unstanzaic verse paragraphs, and with a great deal of enjambement, the poem has obvious affinities both with blank verse and with prose; its prosody is therefore distinctly unlike that of Evgeny Onegin, *with its regular stanzaic form and end-stopped lines. Pushkin's compression of language, his mixture of high style and low, give the poem a verbal density unlike anything in Russian literature, and matched in few other literatures known to me. The "theme" of the poem, which can be described as the conflicting claims and rights of state and individual, is thus heightened by the power and flexibility of the style. This linguistic richness is particularly difficult to approximate in translation: the reader is likely to find more of it, in my version of the poem, if he reads slowly, and still more if he reads aloud.*

The Bronze Horseman:
A Story of Saint Petersburg

[*The Bronze Horseman is a commanding eighteenth-century statue of Tsar Peter the Great (1672–1725), the founder of Saint Petersburg and of the modern Russian state, and the* "HE" *of this poem*]

Prelude

On an empty, wave-washed shore
HE stood in thought,
staring at the far
horizon. The river ran hard
and wide, a battered boat spun on its tide.
Scattered on mossy wet banks
black specks of shelter, huts
of miserable Finns, sank
back into forests shut
from the sun,
and leaves rustled.

    And he thought:
"From here the Swede will be fought,
here we will plant a city
in his haughty
face: fate will set us
a window to Europe, here, let us
stand at the sea. And here,
sailing unknown waves,
ships of a thousand flags will steer
like swallows, and we will play
on the oceans."

A hundred years—

and behold the jewel and wonder of the north,
a proud young city gleaming
where trees grew dark and marshes steamed.
Where the dreary Finn, alone,
ignored,
had roamed
dank mud and caught
what he could, with clumsy nets, in an unknown
river, now towers and palaces push
to the shore, men ride
on boulevards, ships slide
the sea from the ends of the earth, rushing
to high-piled docks;
the Neva is lined with stone,
bridges arch bank to bank across her,
her islands float
dark green with gardens—and old
Moscow blanches,
seen with the young capital—
like a dowager in purple robes
facing a new empress.

I love you, city that Peter made,
I love you severe, graceful,
the Neva flowing through and around you,
king-like, walled in granite,
I love your whorled railings,
your open twilight and the round
silence of moonless nights,
and I reading, writing
with no lamp,
and down deserted streets massed

dark buildings shine,
and the Admiralty spire glows clear
and bright,
and dawn scurries after dawn, sheer
darkness holding night
a bare half hour.
I love the air hung still
and your winter frost,
and sleighs swift on the broad
Neva, and girls' faces brighter
than roses, and shrill
voices swirling, at dancing balls,
and bachelor feasts and foaming
wine and punch warm
in pale-blue flame. I love your soldiers all
in motion, foot and horse, noble, tall,
parading long rows
crisp, in order,
swinging battered banners
and polished bronze helmets, bullet-punctured,
triumphant.
I love, oh city of war,
the booming smoke of your fort,
announcing
a son to the northern
empress or a Russian trouncing
for Russian enemies or ringing
blue ice in the Neva, splitting,
whirling out to sea
as the river smells spring.

Shine, Peter's city,

stand as strong as Russia, let
water and forest
be at peace with you! May waves
rolling from Finland forget
hatred, forget their bondage, let Peter's eternal sleep
be unbroken
by pointless spite!

I remember a horrible time,
a memory like words just spoken . . . . . .
Let me begin
to tell it.
What I tell will be grim.

Part 1

November chill blew
on the dark
city. The Neva threw
grinding waves at her tall stone walls,
rolling, arching
like a sick man tossing in bed.
It was late, black;
rain smashed at the window, a sad
wind howled.
And Evgeny said
his farewells, came home
from his friends . . . . . . let his name
be Evgeny. It sounds
cheerful; I've known
Evgenies, I like the feel on my pen.

Wherever his family came from,
whatever they were called, I feel bound
to ignore, though Karamzin gave them ten
full lines of heroic song—
I may be wrong,
I've forgotten—but so has the world.
Evgeny lives in a slum,
he works at a desk, shuns
aristocrats, has forgotten family banners furled
in dust, and buried baronets.

Home, he threw off his clothes,
lay down.
But his mind leaped about
in the dark, and sleep chose
to lie elsewhere. And what did he think?
That he had no money, that his life
would have to be built, and by him
alone; that it might
be easier with better brains, and more money;
that everything ran well
for lazy, lucky people with funny
grins and dull
heads and useful connections;
that he'd clerked for only two years; that the weather
held,
went no better,
that the Neva was higher,
and the bridges set on
its granite banks
probably raised
and for two or three days

Parasha sealed away
from him—and Evgeny sighed, and sighed,
and dreamed without closing his eyes:

"Suppose—suppose I get married? Why not? But me?
I'd work like a horse—
but I'm strong, I'm healthy,
I can do it, of course
I can—I can make us a little hut,
of course,
and Parasha—Parasha can rest.
And maybe, later, I'll make more money
and Parasha can run
the house—and plenty
of children . . . . . . and life can begin,
go hand in hand to the grave—
and grandchildren will lay us in . . . . . ."
He thought. But his heart ached
and he wished
wind would not blow
like a sad ghost,
rain would not run angry at the pane.
        And at last he closed
his eyes. And darkness scraped
pale into dawn,
and day dragged thinly on—
that ghastly day!

That night the Neva
had fought toward the sea,
and the storm blew back, blew mad,
and the river gave up . . . . . .

at dawn people stood
on her walls, in the spray
and foam, pointing at mountain waves
and gaping.
The mad winds
blew her back on her islands
and the river ran them under—
and then in wind and lightning and thunder
the Neva swelled, roared
like a tiger
gone wild,
and leaped on the city, swirling, huge,
and the city ran,
everything
ran—water in cellars, railings
under water, canals
spinning up,
and Petropolis
turned Triton, standing in a sea.

Battle—siege—
waves like thieves
smashing in windows—boats
cracking glass with their oars—
peddlers' packs, pieces
of huts, roofs, beams,
boxes from shops, tables,
chairs, bridges washed away, stables,
coffins swimming like trees—
everything floating down streets!

And the people wait

for death: God is angry!
The world is over! Houses—food—
too late!

The old Emperor still lived,
ruled;
he stared sadly
from his balcony:
"No Tsar can give
orders to God." He sat
and stared at the flood,
sad, sad.
Plazas were ponds, lakes—
streets came racing
down, pouring, broad.
The palace soared
like an island!
And the Tsar's orders
sent soldiers
sailing in his city, along
every street, risking
lives, saving lives, collecting the fear-stricken
and drowning.

And in Peter's Square
at a corner where a porch
stands high,
graced with marching marble lions—
there,
on a lion, motionless, his head bare,
his arms crossed, Evgeny rides
pale over the flood,

afraid—
but not for himself.
The waves muddy
at his feet—the rain sweeping in his face—
the wind lashing, howling—
he heard nor saw nor felt,
but only stared,
desperate, there
in the distance, there where
waves rose and fell like mountains,
wind screamed,
pieces of the city seemed
to bob like corks—
oh Lord, Lord!
There, near the shore,
near the water,
was her mother's tiny old hut;
Parasha, his dream—
but which
was the dream,
that or this?
Was anything what it seemed,
everything empty, Heaven's joke?
And like something bewitched
he sits yoked
to his marble beast! Water:
everything water, everywhere.
Only water. But reared up high,
untouchable, back turned,
the Rider
on his bronze horse stretches an arm
across a mad, wrecked world.

Part 2

And tired,
sated,
the Neva withdrew—
relishing chaos
but indifferent to new
treasure. Like rioting
bandits, raiding
a village, smashing, cutting, raping—
howling violence, screaming,
foul!
Lugging booty they run,
exhausted, dropping plunder
all down the road, leaving
everything, afraid.

The water ebbed, streets
emerged, and Evgeny—hoping,
grieving, afraid—ran
to the river, still swollen,
full.
Waves bubbled proud,
high,
as though fire
burned in them; the Neva foamed
like a stallion
racing out of war.
Evgeny watched, saw
a boat, and blinking
at a miracle, hailed
the ferryman, set sail

for a price in pennies, thinking
of Parasha, not waves.

And the boatman, afraid
of nothing, slowly wedged
through the water, almost
drowned them, edged
closer and closer—
and finally brought them to shore.

    Evgeny, shaking,
staggered on familiar streets, then ran,
seeing nothing he knew,
all of it heartbreaking—
streets half levelled, torn
apart, ruins
scattered up and down, houses
twisted like balloons, houses flattened,
houses gone, and corpses
everywhere, lying in the mud.
His head battered
with sudden
pain, Evgeny ran where a sealed letter,
signed by Fate,
was waiting
unopened. He ran near the water,
near the road,
near the house . . . . . . near
what house?
He stopped, went back, told
himself: here,
it was here, walked slowly

and looked: here,
here was the willow, their willow.
The gates stood here. What gates?
There were gates. No gates.
What house?
He muttered to himself, loud,
walked, looked—then crashed
his fist to his head, and laughed.

The city slept, dark.
afraid—
but some could not sleep, talked
through the night, remembering that day.

Pale shreds of cloud
opened into morning:
the city lay still, shrouded, now,
in calm, everything
swept and cleared
at the Tsar's orders,
at the Tsar's expense.
Work began,
clerks strolled,
indifferent, to their desks.
Officials managed
to clean their uniforms, scold
their wives, and get to their desks.
Peddlers opened their stalls,
cursing the river
but knowing their neighbors would pay,
in time. Boats were hauled
away. And Khvostov, bard

of society, poured out
verses on disaster.

But Evgeny! My poor
Evgeny . . . . . . his mind
could not hold, spun,
roared. The running
waves echoed in his ears,
and the wind. Time
broke, his brain rehearsed
terror, he lived in a dream.
Silent, he roamed
a week, a month, forgot home.
Unseen,
he passed for dead.
The landlord rented his bed
to a poet. And Evgeny left
everything, walked through the world
a stranger. At night he slept
near the river: from dawn to sunset
he walked, aimless,
fed
by scraps pushed through windows.
His clothes were rotted, mouldy, ripped.
Children hit him
with stones. Coachmen whipped him,
he was always lost,
in the way, not knowing,
not seeing. An inner roar
stuffed his ears.
A year
passed, he was fish nor fowl, not man,

not beast, a miserable phantom,
neither dead nor alive.
                              One night
he slept near the Neva. Summer
grew cold, autumn came close. A foul wind rumbled,
waves lapped at the walls,
weary, slapping on the steps,
grumbling
like a prisoner calling
for mercy, but ignored.
He woke up. It was dark,
rain dripped, wind roared
heavily, watchmen barked
in the night . . . . . . Evgeny shook
remembering floods and terror.
He rose, took
some wandering
steps—then stopped,
trembling, his eyes wide.
He stood beside
that porch;
the huge lions
marched
on guard—
and mounted on living rock,
huger still, dark,
the Rider
stretched out his arm, rode his bronze horse.
                              He shivered.
His mind cleared.
This was where the river
had crowded streets,

angry, sprung loose—this was where
he had sat on lions,
in this plaza, and that Rider
had held his bronze head high
in the darkness, he
who had built this city by the sea . . . . . .
He sat monstrous in the half
light—planning
God knew what behind
those cold bronze eyes!
Hiding fantastic power! Riding that horse!
Where? Galloping where, oh Master
of Fate? Standing
on the edge of nothing, you forced
Russia to climb
in the air, like this, like this, with your iron
whip!

Evgeny came round the Rider, stood staring
at his face,
glaring
at the emperor of his world.
His chest went stiff,
his face pressed on the railings,
darkness held his eyes, his fists
tightened, his blood burned,
his heart flamed,
sullen, and biting his jaw
he quivered with rage—
and whispered as though calling
to the devil, "All right, you marvellous city-maker!
Just wait!"

And suddenly he raced
away.
The Tsar's metal face
flared, burning
with anger. He felt it turning . . . . . .
and he stumbled
across the plaza, hearing behind him,
like thunder rumbling,
hooves clanging on stone,
faster, faster, grinding
fire from the quivering road.
Lit by a pale moon, his hand
reaching high, the Bronze Horseman
rushed wildly after him; all night
Evgeny ran
and the Rider came clanging
after on his massive
stallion, galloping fast.

Evgeny could never approach
the statue,
never, without a sad,
bewildered pain showing
in his face. He'd press
his hand to his heart, where it hurt, raise
his cap, lower his eyes, and go
some slow
circuitous way.

A small island in the Neva
where fishermen out late
moor and float

and hurriedly eat;
on Sundays
petty officials come boating,
stop to explore.
Nothing grows
on the rock, not a blade
of grass. An empty, deserted place.
The flood had played
with a battered hut, lifted it, left it
like a black bush. It stayed
till spring, was dragged away
in a barge. A ruined, empty old wreck.
Evgeny's corpse lay
at its door: they dug his grave
where they found him, and there he lies.

Baron Anton Antonovitch Delvig: 1798–1831

PUSHKIN'S SCHOOLMATE and closest friend, Delvig developed early and wrote little; he was equally famous for his wisdom, his kindness, and his laziness. Technically a master, he perfected the epigram and was the first Russian poet to fully domesticate the sonnet. He functioned as editor of a yearly miscellany, and just before his death had been given permission to publish a *Literary Gazette*. (See also under Baratynsky, below.)

Death

Death, soul's comfort!
Will you fly down
to tell me this pleasant life is over
while I sleep, while I'm awake?
Will you puff out my little candle
in the daytime, or at night,
letting me take instead
your neverworldly light?

But no eternal contracts
in the morning: please.
The muse is with me, mornings,
we write together—leave us in peace.
Nor at dinner: no invitations:
Why frighten my friends?
I love them like food,
like my cheerful poems.

And my evenings go to other muses,
to Bacchus, to my friends.
But in the quiet night,
yes, then we can be together:
silent on my bed,
grieving for love,
waiting in vain
while darkness slips away.

Cupid: a sonnet

Cupid coming to Spain is no guest,
is at home, not strange, known to his friends;
castanets click as he sings a festive
love song and dances with Spanish zest.

His passion lights fires in a lovely cheek,
her heart heats, her lips burn
and her eyes flare—as the myrtle
and orange blow and wave and turn.

But he comes to the north, sometimes, comes easy
and gay; he feels a concern for our climate;
and isn't it Cupid who's put that neat

Line of teeth in your mouth, lit
those large eyes, reddened your lips,
and given you powers that whirl my wits?

Death: an aphorism

I've no fear of death, just regret
at losing my body—
who likes replacing a pleasant,
worn old robe?

Evgeny Abramovitch Baratynsky: 1800–1844

SENT TO AN aristocratic military school at age twelve, Baratynsky was almost at once expelled for theft and made to serve in the ranks. He was rallied, even perhaps "saved," by the kindness and help of Delvig, who praised his writing and saw to it that some of Baratynsky's early poems were published. Transferred to Finland in 1820, Baratynsky there began to write fully mature work and acquired a substantial literary reputation. Commissioned, at last, in 1825, Baratynsky retired from the army the next year.

Of a melancholy cast, a superb craftsman—precise, dry, brilliant—Baratynsky is at the same time clearly indebted to Pushkin and also clearly his own man. Without Pushkin's example, it is very unlikely that he would have written his three narrative poems, but they are distinctly unlike Pushkin, coolly sentimental, consciously detailed and realistic. Less fluent than Pushkin's, less charismatic, his verse is classical, often intellectual, witty (though not humorous). He was not particularly popular in his own time.

Baratynsky died in Naples, of tuberculosis, while in the course of a journey through France and Italy.

The Muse

My Muse does not dazzle:
no one weeps at her beauty,
boys do not leave their duty
to pursue her in a panting
mob. She cannot and does not seduce
with her clothes, or the choice
flirting of her eyes, or her witty
talk, but sometimes, for a bit,
the world notices her strange face,
her quiet voice,
and instead of vicious criticism
grants her some casual, passing praise.

What Good Are You, Days?

What good are you, days?
The world changes
nothing, everything is known
and will stay
the same.

Soul, you twisted and boiled
as you grew:
you knew
fulfillment faster than this toiling
body, dull and soiled.

Your frenzy ran you around
the world's small circle that you found
barren; you've slipped
into dreams that fit
your soaring boundaries,

While the body stares as day follows night.
Each aimless evening
sinks from light,
from meaning—
emptiness its cherished height!

Inspiration

I love you, goddesses of song,
but your magic that crashes
delicate as waves, that flashes
bright in my heart, turns life all wrong.

Your love and Fate's
curses come together. I'm afraid
to sing, my fingers
light on the strings
might shake disaster's sleep.

Desperate, I break
away from my Muse:
"Tomorrow, music;
let today die without waking."

Mikhail Yurievitch Lermontov: 1814–1841

Of distantly scots ancestry, Lermontov was raised, and atrociously spoiled, by his maternal grandmother (his mother died when he was three, and his grandmother spirited him away). He began writing, mostly in imitation of Byron, at age thirteen; like Byron, also, he was all his life intensely self-conscious and hypersensitively vain. "He was physically of smallish stature, with velvety eyes, broad shoulders and bowlegs" (Lermontov, *A Hero of Our Time*, trans. Vladimir Nabokov, p. 202, n. 53). After two years at Moscow University (1830–1832), Lermontov abruptly left, went to Saint Petersburg and, though intending to enroll in the university there, entered cadet school and graduated, in 1834, with a commission in the Hussars of the Guard.

Playing the role to the hilt (though, it seems, not much enjoying it), Lermontov seemed to have become a typical coarse, whoring, socialite officer—but on Pushkin's death, in 1837, he burst out with a passionate poetic denunciation of Russian society for permitting, even encouraging, the death of so great a writer. Lermontov was promptly arrested, tried, and exiled to the Caucasus, but after a year was allowed to return. Now a literary lion, he began to publish widely, though he rejected literary society. In 1840 he fought a duel, for no very good reason, with the son of the French ambassador, and was again exiled. He turned out to be a brilliant soldier and was several times recommended for official recognition, each time denied to him by the authorities in Saint Petersburg. In 1841 he picked another senseless duel, this time with an old schoolmate. He was killed at once. (There is some speculation that the duel was arranged by the Tsarist government, as a way of eliminating Lermontov, but this has not been proven. Similar speculations exist as to Pushkin's duel with d'Anthès.)

Pushkin was desperately unhappy in Russian society, but never alone. Lermontov was always essentially alone, in society and in literature. Pushkin's lifetime was at least in part coterminous with the so-called Golden Age of Russian poetry; Lermontov's lifetime coincided with one of the nadirs of Russian poetry. "Throughout his whole life he tried to become 'like everyone else,' and his behavior was always distorted by straining and artificiality" (Slonim, *The Epic of Russian Literature*, p. 112). In Pushkin's formative years he studied from French models; Lermontov belonged to a different generation, was not steeped in French Enlightenment values, and began as simply an overflowing young Romantic, vague, even incoherent. Much of Lermontov's verse, accordingly, and virtually all his early works, is rant and rhetoric. (His juvenilia were published only after his death, and unfortunately comprise the bulk of his literary corpus.) In his last years, however, Lermontov did in fact become the recognized successor of Pushkin, his style now clearly derived from, even an extension of Pushkin's.

I'm on the Road

I'm on the road, alone:
mist shines on the stone;
the silent forest listens to God,
star whispers to star;

The sky hangs dark and high,
a pale blue earth lies
asleep . . . . . . and I?
So heavy, so sad? Waiting? Regretting?

But not expecting: life
has nothing to give, had nothing
to give: and all I need
is nothingness, its freedom, its peace . . . . . .

But not the grave: the sleep
I want is eternal, with breath
slow in my lungs, life still deep
in my heart,

So songs of love can bewitch
my ear, and a ravishing voice,
and a dark green oak forever twitch
its leaves, rustling above me.

January First

In the middle of a jabbering mob,
an ape-like masquerade—
noble—parading
like a nightmare, slobbering
to music, prancing, whispering speeches
stolen from books—
when courtly bitches
with steady hands stroke
my wrists, unblinking, indifferent—
then I laugh their games, blow
their puff balls, but send
my soul to a buried dream, a moment
of remembering, fly
in a soft free haze
back to days
destroyed, now. My eye
sees a child, me,
a great old house, a garden, glassed-in plants,
a pond misted with grass,
a village, smoke drifting high,
dew rising from the fields.
I walk under huge elms, one slice
of twilight on the bushes, yellow leaves
shifting at my quiet feet.
And a lovely sadness heaves
in my heart : I weep
for her, loving my dream
with sky-blue eyes and a smile
like sunrise on trees.
And I sat alone
for hours, king on a fairy throne—
and while

I live I remember, in spite of storms
and doubt; I keep a tiny island green
in an ocean desert. But returning,
remembering, mob-noise screaming my dream
away—my quiet unknown guest—
I burn
to break their laughter, splash them
with bitter lines, and passion . . . . . . !

How Bored I Am

How bored, how depressed I am—and who
would take my hand if I reached it out?
Longing! What good is empty longing?
And time slides by—all the best years!
Love? Who? Why bother, for a night?
And no one loves forever.
Nothing lasts, the past is gone
forever—the pain, the delight, everything
worthless . . . . . . passion? It evaporates too,
eventually; a breath of thought—puff!
And life, if you really look at it,
is such a dull, such an empty farce . . . . . .

Song

When ripe corn bends in the wind,
and cool woods sing,
and red plums in the garden
hang in a dark-leaf ring;

When rose-drawn twilight or yellow
dawn open a silvered lilly
(damp with dew) to a mellow
smile, and hilly

Slopes sparkle with springs—
I refuse to think,
my ears hear ancient songs
of lands where rivers belong;

Then fear is silent,
my forehead calm,
happiness no violent
dream, and Heaven holds God.

The Dream

in 1841, a few months before his death
(in a pistol duel with a fellow officer
at the foot of Mount Mashuk, in the
Caucasus), Mikhail Lermontov composed a
prophetic poem . . . . . .
    VLADIMIR NABOKOV,
    Translator's Foreword, *A Hero of*
    Our Time

Burning noon, a valley in Daghestan,
on my back, a bullet in my heart; still;
the bloody hole steaming, my blood
oozing drop by drop.

Alone on the sand, rocks and cliffs
above me, burning yellow
in the sun, the sun burning me,
but I asleep as if dead.

And dreaming of a ball, torches
and candles, in Russia,
and girls hung with flowers
laughing, talking about me.

But one girl sad, silent,
sitting alone, dreaming
God knows why
a miserable dream

Of a valley in Daghestan
where a familiar corpse steamed
with blood flowing
and slowly chilling cold . . . . . .

4.

From Tyutchev
to Annensky

Fyodor Ivanovitch Tyutchev: 1803–1873

A NOBLEMAN, a diplomat (he lived abroad for some twenty years), in later life an arch conservative, speaking and reading mostly French (neither of his two wives spoke Russian), Tyutchev is one of Russia's great lyric poets. His best poetry falls into two main periods: first, the decade 1830 to 1840 (to which period belongs "Silentium," here translated), and second, the decade 1854 to 1864, during which years he had a passionate, tortured love affair with his daughter's governess (to which period belong "Final Love" and "Those Eyes," here translated). The governess died, miserably unhappy, in 1864. Tyutchev thereafter became almost desperately active in politics, and wrote a good deal of political verse. (In the 1850s he had been chairman of foreign censorship; he held a variety of high posts in the Foreign Office.) Much of Tyutchev's earlier poetry was published by Pushkin himself; it went largely unnoticed. It was only in 1854, when he collected his poetry in a volume, that his reputation was established.

Silentium

Be silent, hide,
keep feelings
and dreams hidden, sealed
in your heart like silent
stars : watch them, admiring,
smiling, and be still.

Can the heart talk?
Who could understand it?
Who knows why you live? Mawkish
words tell lies, not thoughts;
swimming in a river stains it:
just drink, and be still.

Learn how to live in your mind :
a world of ideas whirls
in your soul; the noise outside
drowns them; daylight withers
their songs : listen
as they sing, and be still.

Dreams

As the ocean circles the shore
our life is surrounded by dreams.
Night—and their heavy waves
ring like great bells against our earth.

Like a voice, forcing, inviting . . . . . .
An enchanted canoe is tied at the dock,
the tide swells, we whirl away
in an endless dark sea.

And the gleaming high sky
watches, somewhere, silent—
and on we sail, on every side
a flaming abyss.

Twilight

Blue gray shadows fuse,
light fades, silence spreads—
all life, all motion turn
to hesitant twilight, to faraway noise . . . . . .
a moth's invisible wings
hum in the night air . . . . . .
oh hour of incredible pain!
Everything in me, I in it all . . . . . .

Oh quiet twilight, restful twilight,
pour down my soul,
silent, lazy, fragrant,
flood me, calm me,
fill me with the mist
of not-knowing . . . . . .
let me taste the nothing,
fuse me in a world of sleep.

Night Wind

Night wind, why howl?
Why grumble so madly?
Why this strange song,
toneless and sad, then loud and harsh?
The heart understands you
as you sing, over and over, some terrible torture—
but you dig at the heart, you roll and revel in it,
and it shouts and sometimes it screams! . . . . . .
Oh, not those wild songs
of ancient chaos!
The soul's night-world hangs, greedy,
on every syllable of its favorite story.
It leaps from our breasts,
it longs to blend with that endlessness! . . . . . .
Oh, leave those storms asleep:
underneath them the chaos heaves and waits.

Final Love

Oh how we love at the end,
how deep, how afraid . . . . . .
Glow, glow, last light
of my final love, oh sunset!

The sky is drawn with shadows,
only a flicker, there in the west:
wait, slow, evening glow,
stay, stay, oh magic.

Blood runs thinner in the veins
but the heart is as hot . . . . . .
Oh final love, oh desperation
and delight!

Those Eyes

Those eyes, those eyes!
I loved them—more, more!
My soul hung
on their glowing night.

Eyes so deep
that they reached to beginning and end,
opened life,
and sorrow, and Love

That quivered sad
in the shadow of a lash, exhausted
like pleasure, sister
of suffering and as mortal.

Eyes never met
marvellously
without tears
of delight.

Karolina Karenovna Pavlova (née Jaenisch) 1807–1893

PAVLOVA WAS OF German ancestry; Soviet critics are fond of pointing out the Slavophile aspects of her work. The two central events in her life were an early affair with Adam Mickiewicz (1798–1855), the Polish writer exiled to Russia from 1824 to 1829, and her subsequent unhappy marriage to a minor novelist, Nicholas F. Pavlov (1805–1864). Her passion for Mickiewicz never died.

Pavlova wrote novels, as well as poetry; the best known is *The Double Life* (1848). She translated Schiller, and also translated A. K. Tolstoy from Russian into German. Her Moscow literary salon was very well frequented, though she herself was not much appreciated by her contemporaries, either personally or professionally. Her reputation stands considerably higher today: she is generally considered the leading Russian woman poet of the nineteenth century.

"Rome," here translated, was written in 1857. It should be understood that for an adherent of the Russian Orthodox Church, Rome represents a deeply decadent, corrupting world force. In Dostoyevsky's *The Brothers Karamazov*, the Grand Inquisitor, who is a Roman Catholic Cardinal, "claims it [reports Ivan Karamazov] as a merit for himself and his Church that at last they have vanquished freedom and have done so to make men happy." The Cardinal goes on to tell Christ, "We are not working with Thee, but with *him*—that is our mystery. . . . Just eight centuries ago . . . we took from him Rome and the sword of Caesar, and proclaimed ourselves sole rulers of the earth, though hitherto we have not been able to complete our work" (pp. 298, 305).

My Soul Aches

My soul aches, thinking numbly of what was,
what died, what is gone, gone.
I've seen too much blackness,
I've wasted too much of my heart,
given too much and gotten too little.

And every time I tried
again, blundered innocent into the world,
forgot what I'd learned, what I'd paid for:
my heart refused to abandon
its trust in tears, in words, in laughter.

My soul never accepted its fate,
my soul was sure it could win
in the end, in spite of hard luck,
and sat day after day waiting
for a change, like a gambler waiting out a game.

All my chips were thrown down, one after another,
fearlessly, until there was nothing.
And now the lucky ones on either side of me
watch greedily, sourly, wondering
if my heart will weaken, if I will go under.

The Streets Are Silent

The streets are silent. It's late.
The sky arches black,
clouds assemble like armies,
like soldiers marching at an enemy.

I watch those dark battles
from my window
and remember—I should not remember—
other days,

Only a few, but days
when for hours
I waited for a doorbell,
I thought I heard a doorbell.

And nothing came, nothing!
And even now
am I not permitted to forget it all,
that whole old fairy-tale?

I am calm, I am content,
the madness has passed . . . . . .
but something still hurts,
something still presses on me.

Rome

Open country, our carriage
alone;
clouds in the distance, and a stone
city.

Thunder calls it,
rattles its name,
the dark sky rolls,
flames.

City in a desert, a silent
jungle, city alone,
king with no throne,
damned by his sins,

Sick, helpless, gray,
staring
at the waste
all around him

Where his messengers ran
to the world, brought news
and laws, life and death,
and his soldiers camped,

And kings bowed low. Sand
sweeps in the wind,
mist rises gray
from the swamps.

Count Alexey Konstantinovitch Tolstoy 1817–1875

A. K. TOLSTOY, a childhood friend of Tsar Alexander II, and a distant cousin of Lev Nikoleyevitch Tolstoy, is best known as a historical dramatist and novelist, and also as a humorous poet, perhaps the greatest of Russian humorous poets. He wrote narrative poems and ballads of interest but no great distinction, and lyrics (after about 1854) which are sometimes sentimental, sometimes singularly clear, open, honest—almost Japanese in their purity. He is in no way an innovator in his serious poetry; his style is eclectic; but his sensibility is fine and in the very best sense harmonious.

My Carriage Bumps and Rumbles

My carriage bumps and rumbles
on a dam hung
with dripping fish-nets;
I sit and dream,

Watching the gray day,
grass sloping to a lake,
the winding road, haze
and smoke near a village.

A sad Jew in rags
crosses the dam, water
swishes over, foams in jagged
small waves;

A boy in the rushes
whistles his reed pipe;
ducks are frightened
and fly and cry;

Peasants at a sagging mill
rest in the dust,
and a tired old horse shuffles
with a cart . . . . . .

I've seen it, not here,
but somewhere before:
roofs in the dull glare,
the boy, the trees, the lake,

The millstone grumbling slow,
that broken barn—
I've seen it before, far
away and forgotten.

A horse plodded the same slow track,
his cart was loaded with those dirty sacks,
the peasants flopping in the dust
were the same, and the mill,

And the Jew and his beard came by,
and the water sang.
I've seen it before—but I,
I cannot remember . . . . . .

When All the World Trembles

When all the world trembles and glows,
colored bright and colored hot,
the soul drowns, lazy,
and splits in a million sweet, soft shafts.
But in quiet, cool autumn,
when the air is gray and no one sees far,
nature no longer splits me apart,
it cannot push me aside.
My mind stays sober, inspiration sweeps in,
I live deep inside myself,
compressed dreams call up crowds of visions—
as if sparking them out with a flame.
I lift my rifle from the wall, leave the house
and walk a blackening road, between winter crops;
I watch haystacks, a broken fence,
the pond and the windmill, the wild horizon,
the creek's marshy, sloping shore,
and I turn into the forest next door. A maple, gone red.
An oak, still green. Yellow birches.
And they all shake their tears down on me.
But I walk on, deep in dreams,
half-bare branches drooping over my head,
my thoughts slowly turning into harmonies,
words pushing into shape, taking names,
my heart light, and sweet, and strange,
and everything quiet around me, and under my foot
the wet, soft rustle of the leaves.

Sometimes, in the Middle of Daily Things

Sometimes, in the middle of daily things, pressed, worried,
some painful thought
tears your face from my soul.
But when I can be alone, quiet,
when the day is done, is still,
then all that unreal anguish fades,
my soul turns clear, transparent as a lake,
and I can stare down to its bottom—
and in that calm thought, disturbed by nothing,
I see your image, my belovèd,
and I see those clear sands where, like some glittering treasure,
my love lies waiting for you.

Yakov Petrovitch Polonsky: 1819–1898

OF A PROSPEROUS noble (but not aristocratic) family, Polonsky attended Moscow University and graduated as a lawyer. In addition to working as a censor, he served for a brief period as editor of the magazine, *The Russian Word*.

Polonsky was naturally Romantic but, like many Russians, was bent away from full exploration of his sensibility by his liberal/progressive insistence on the social utility of literature. Much of his work—and he was very popular in his lifetime—deals with the virtues of progress, the value of free speech, and so on. His play, *Discord* (1864), was written to criticize the 1863 Polish revolt against Russian domination. Polonsky also wrote fiction, verse for children, and a popular humorous poem, "The Grasshopper Musician" (1859). His more purely Romantic verse shows affinities with that of Lermontov, and resemblances to Russian folklore.

The Soviet view is that, from 1880 to 1890, Polonsky began to succumb to "reactionary" feelings, aligning himself with such currently disfavored writers as Fet; this "estheticism," this art-for-art's-sake "decadence," concentrated on nature, love, and Romance, rather than on social subjects. But even Soviet criticism concedes Polonsky's lyricism—which was also recognized by composers like Tchaikovsky, Taneyev, and Anton Rubinstein, who set his poetry to music. Eclectic rather than original, Polonsky has a very real lyric gift.

The Swan

Lights in the park, people
walking, a violin;
only the wind asleep,
the sky dark.

And the pond dark, and the rushes
where a swan was hiding,
thick rushes, quiet
night.

Tame, alone, dying,
he could not see rockets
bursting into fire
above him,

Nor hear the fountain, or the brook;
eyes closed
he dreamed a soaring flight
where his wings shook

Clouds, carried him high
in a wide sky—
and the songs he sang!
Sacred things

No man had found
would echo from crowds
of white swans, resound
soaring, loud.

And he dreamed a sigh,
his wings flying,
his song proclaiming
morning.

But nothing moved.
The song broke in his mind.
He lay dying
and still in the half light.

A breeze blew,
leaves rustled in the dark;
lights in the park,
and a violin.

Another Winter

I remember us as red–cheeked children
running together in brittle snow:
winter caressed us kindlily, with its shaggy arms,
and waving its crutch herded us to a warm fire.
And later that night your round little eyes would shine,
and the small flame flickering in the stove would watch,
as our old nurse told us fairy–stories
about how, once upon a time, there was a tiny fool.

But May smiled that winter away from us,
and then the summer cooled away—and now, after the sound
of autumn howling, we have another winter coming,
with no kindness, a cruel winter, threatening with its crutch.

And our old nurse has uncurled her feet
and sleeps soundly in her grave and can't see
how you, weary, cling to my arms
as if trying to hear my heart.
And so my heart, warm to a child's caress,
like our old dead nurse, blows on the small fire
and whispers fairy–stories in your ear,
about how, once upon a time, there was a tiny fool.

Night-Shadows

Night-shadows glide to my door,
stand there on guard!
Her eyes' blue darkness stare
hard into mine,
her voice hangs in a whisper over my ear,
and my hand crumples her hair, curls it
like a snake, waves it into my face.

Wait, night! Fold down on love's enchanted world
with your thick darkness.
Time, with your feeble old hand,
hold back your clock.

But night-shadows sway, stagger,
and run fading away.
Her eyes turn down,
stay down, see without seeing:
her hand grows cold in mine,
her face slips down on my breast—
oh sun, sun! Wait a little longer!

My Song

My song is watching for sunrise,
waiting to flow like a stream:
oh not the dark night, but the burning east
color it, glow in it!
Let birds whistle as they please,
let the forest stir and wake and run,
and the owl—let it not hoot in my ears,
let it sit, with its blind eyes, in some different place, not too near.

Afanasy Afanasyevitch Fet (Shenshin) 1820–1892

BORN OF a landowning family, but one which was not of noble status, Fet attended university and in 1841 enlisted in the army. He served for fifteen years, trying with almost painful determination to attain a rank which would (as was then the law in Russia) automatically confer noble status. When he had finally managed that, Fet retired to his small country estate (which was near L. N. Tolstoy's: the two became close friends). He was technically illegitimate, since his father's marriage to a German woman (whose name was Fet) had taken place abroad and was considered invalid under Russian law. His father's family name was Shenshin, but Fet was unable to use this name until, in 1876, the Tsar issued a special decree granting him that right. Fet never used his father's name for his literary work, however, and though he is sometimes referred to, now, as "Shenshin-Fet," neither he nor his contemporaries so described him.

The discomforts and strains of his early years led Fet to an increasingly fixed attitude of withdrawal. As a mature man, he was notorious for his reserved, guarded manner, which both seemed, and at times really was, simple indifference. His political views happened to be reactionary, but politics did not concern him; it is significant that he could remain on close friendly terms with both Turgenev (expatriate, aristocrat) and Tolstoy (worshipper of Mother Russia and Her peasants), although Turgenev and Tolstoy's own relationship quickly became distant and on the whole rather unpleasant. Fet's poetry, too, tends to be intensely self-absorbed, pure, at least in part, by virtue of its indifference to issues which do not concern it. His themes are love, nature, and death; it has been argued that he is able to write about these subjects with fervor, often with remarkable fervor, precisely because of his long history of sublimation and outright repression. In his translations, too, which are considered extremely fine, Fet chose work which was either classical and controlled (Horace, Goethe) or, if more Romantic, then Romantic in rather abstracted ways (Schopenhauer—who was his favorite philosopher).

Fet was never prolific. Radical attacks on his estheticism, his personal politics, and also on his personality, led him to stop publishing for twenty years, from 1863 to 1883. Although he wrote during that time, public hostility did also interfere with his ability to work. In 1870, for example, Turgenev wrote to a mutual friend: "Fet has really become rather strange; he writes me very long and, to tell the truth, unintelligible letters; the only thing apparent is that something is constantly irritating him. I submit that in no way has he been able to reconcile himself with the termination of his literary work. We shall have to try, and calm him down somewhat" (*Turgenev's Letters*, p. 224). Turgenev did not fully appreciate Fet's poetry. Tolstoy did—but what he almost casually calls Fet's "artless" verse is plainly something dearly bought and incessantly paid for. (Tolstoy made the remark in a conversation with Maxim Gorky. See his *Reminiscences of Tolstoy, Chekhov, and Andreyev*, p. 7.)

Fet ranks among the very greatest of Russian lyricists, with a voice distinctly his own. Soviet critics tend to mention him only for condemnatory purposes; he is neither taught nor read in Soviet schools.

On a Southern Night

On a southern night, on my back
in the hay, and stars
circled in the sky, black
and light, alive like choirs—

And the earth, as dumb as a dream,
ran and was blind,
and I like Adam seemed
alone with the night:

Was I running to that emptiness in the sky?
Was it running to me?
A hand held me high
above infinity,

And my heart spun and whirled
as I stared down
where nothing rose and swirled
around me, spun up and around.

Here I Am

Here I am
to tell you the sun
is born and burning
hot in the leaves;

To tell you the forest
is awake and wet
with spring thirst, and birds
are singing everywhere;

To tell you my love
is as it was,
ready for happiness,
ready for you;

To tell you that joy
breathes from the earth—
and what will I sing?
A song, a song.

Dark Sky

Dark sky, and thunder,
sea sounds roaring—
thunder in the waves,
and my mind roaring—
my mind roaring
and the sea sounds, sea sounds—
black clouds, my mind,
the sound of an angry sea.

Spring Will Be Coming

Open, blowing spring
will be coming, but now
the hills are covered with snow
and at dawn the cart comes clattering
on a frozen road.

The noon sun is cold,
the lime tree glows red,
birches stand in a yellow
line, the nightingale crouches
in a bush, afraid of its song.

But the cranes are flying
and spring will come
and a girl watches the sky
full of swift birds, her eyes
wide, glowing like the cold sun.

Amphitrité

Ah, Amphitrité! daughter of the sea,
how your garland gleams in the sun's first light!
How the sky burns, white
with molten mother of pearl!

Seaweed coiled without end
splashes on the sand,
and the arch of the world bends
in the water, glows like a rose.

Above the green shade: an island, now.
Nothing moves. No sound.
Rushes sway at the waves, bend low,
beaded in drops of dew.

Like Gnats at Dawn

Like gnats at dawn
these sounds hum together;
the heart wants to keep
its favorite dream.

But the bloom of inspiration
droops among daily thorns;
the impulse is somewhere
far away, like a twilight reflection.

And memory, memory
crawls nervously to the heart . . . . . .
Oh, if the soul
could speak without words!

Nikolai Alexeyevitch Nekrasov: 1821–1877

BORN INTO A noble family of modest but adequate means, Nekrasov became his time's leading poet of the Left—as Fet was the leading poet of the Right. (The two men were, however, mutually respectful, even friendly; they visited Italy together, in 1856.) Often genuinely radical, often a man of (or at least passionately devoted to) the people, Nekrasov was also a self-made millionaire, a gambler, a hard drinker, a Rabelaisian eater, a wild rake, and an unscrupulous, driving businessman-publisher. He was capable of eulogizing a tyrannical Tsarist general, in a poem, in order to try to escape (unsuccessfully) governmental repression of his magazine. Consumed by guilt, he could never forgo the things which left him guilt-ridden. "Nekrasov's love of the people," concluded Dostoyevsky after the poet's death, "was but *an outlet of his personal sorrow about himself*" (*The Diary of a Writer*, 2, 946). "His was a heart wounded in the very early days of his life, and it was *that wound which never did heal* that was the inception and source of his whole lifelong passionate and suffering poetry" (ibid., p. 936; italics are Dostoyevsky's).

Nekrasov loved his mother—desperately, sentimentally. He talked of her, with tears in his eyes, all his life. His father was quarrelsome, rough, vulgar, abusive of his wife, and tyrannical to his son. When the boy did poorly at school, the older man sent him, at age seventeen, to the army. Nekrasov rebelled; he wanted to attend the university. To bring him to heel, his father abruptly cut him off without a penny, without any means of support whatever.

Nekrasov found himself literally without a kopeck on the streets of St. Petersburg, where for three years he existed as a homeless derelict. His face, puffy from sleepless nights, was swathed in a ragged red muffler, his wrists, crimson from the cold, stuck out from the short sleeves of a tattered violet-hued frock coat. As he confessed later, he "was famished every day for three years." To earn enough for a piece of bread and a slice of sausage he resorted to all sorts of shifts and strategems: by hanging around lodging-houses he made a few kopecks writing letters or filling out legal forms; he did odd jobs in the St. Petersburg slums and felt very fortunate when he was entrusted with making up the posters for a waxworks museum. (Slonim, *The Epic of Russian Literature*, pp. 231–232)

At age twenty, Nekrasov managed to bring out a pamphlet of Lermontov-inspired poems, *Dreams and Sounds*. Not a single copy was sold.

But he wrote so continuously, and with such bitter determination, that after 1841 he began to have, first, minor successes (some comic pieces accepted for staging; an introduction to the critic, and later his intimate friend, V. Belinsky), and then major ones. Working with incredible energy, and with immense skill, he rapidly pyramided his growing literary talents, his extraordinary editorial talents, and his associations with literary men and men of power, into a small publishing empire. By 1846 he was publisher and editor of an important monthly journal *The Contemporary* (*Sovremennik*—founded by Pushkin). There was nothing accidental about his editorial successes.

One May evening in 1845 Dmitry Grigorivitch, a young nobleman, brought a manuscript, written by a friend of his and entitled *Poor Folk*, to Nekrasov, who was about to publish a literary anthology. They read the manuscript aloud. The pathetic story of a humble clerk and his self-sacrificing love made Nekrasov so enthusiastic that he wanted to rush out and make the author's acquaintance forthwith. Grigorivitch objected that the author must be asleep at that late hour. "Who cares?" retorted Nekrasov. "We'll wake him up. This is more important than sleep."

And so, at four o'clock in the morning, they were congratulating and embracing a baffled young man named Fyodor Dostoyevsky. The impression made on the latter by this surprising visit was everlasting. "This was the most delightful moment of all my life," he wrote later. (Ibid., p. 272)

When a young and totally unknown army officer, L. N. Tolstoy, sent him (pseudonymously at that!) his first novel, *Childhood*, Nekrasov rushed it into print and encouraged the unknown to write more. (Tolstoy was so totally unknown that Turgenev, who knew the Tolstoy family, thought that Lev's brother Nikolai had written *Childhood*.) Nekrasov's editorial energy and skill were such that "He succeeded in attracting the contributions of the greatest writers of the period, so that each issue of the monthly was a genuine literary event. . . . For many years, as editor and promotor of periodicals, he practically shaped a whole body of public opinion" (ibid., pp. 233–234). "Nekrasov was an editor of genius: his ability to get the best literature and to find the right man to write on current subjects was marvellous" (Mirsky, *A History of Russian Literature*, p. 239).

But Nekrasov is still more important, and far more permanently cherished, as a poet. He wrote far too much; much of what he wrote is trifling, silly. "Much of his poetry is excessively sentimental and rhetorical," notes Dmitri Obolensky (*The Penguin Book of Russian Verse*, p. xviii). But he is one of the greatest in a long line of Russian civic poets, deeply committed to the view that writers should "serve the great aims of the age." A vigorous realist, he remained closely in touch with natural as well as social reality: his great satiric poem, *Who is Happy in Russia?*, is an unrhymed epic with a social canvas worthy of *The Canterbury Tales*, while his *Frost the Red-Nosed* features an "incomparable description of the enchantment of the frozen forest" (ibid., p. xliii). A determined experimenter, too, he was particularly successful at the chancy and difficult art of crossing high literate styles with the traditional poetry of the people. "Drawing upon peasant songs, using formalistic preambles, deliberate repetitions, parallels, negative similes, and other devices of folklore, Nekrasov built all his poetry on the rhythms and structural peculiarities of the ballads—the recitative and oral heritage of Central Russia" (Slonim, *The Epic of Russian Literature*, p. 239). He was rarely a finished, polished artist in the aristocratic sense—which accounts for Turgenev's remark, in an 1868 letter, that "Nekrasov is a poet of strainings and tricks. I tried to read his collected poems again a few days ago. No! Poetry did not even spend a night there —and I threw that chewed-up papier-mache with its strong vodka sauce into the corner" (*Turgenev's Letters*, p. 173). Turgenev was an aristocrat first and forever; it is easy to understand his irritated impatience with Nekrasov's often uncertain taste, his contempt for a supposedly "high" artist who drew so heavily on the "low" styles. "But the inspiration," says Mirsky much more justly, "the sheer poetic energy of many of even his most questionable poems, is so great that one has to accept the occasional bathos as an ingredient of the whole" (*A History of Russian Literature*, p. 240). For all his romanticism, Turgenev could not have helped, further, feeling a deep mistrust for Nekrasov's perpetual *andante lacrimoso* tone, the quavers and sobs of an operatic tenor carried to an almost obsessive extreme. " 'He wept more effectively and beautifully than any other Russian poet,' remarked Chukovsky; he sobbed over the sad fate of the peasants and over his own 'broken life,' over his mother, over Belinsky, over the wives of the Decembrists. His mellifluous verse, drawling with dactylic endings and prolonged vowels, sounds like a solo in a choir—a slow, mournful voice repeating his complaint. . . ." (Slonim, *The Epic of Russian Literature*, p. 238). With real revulsion Turgenev said of *Vlas*—a poem to which I shall return, in a moment—that "It would have been better if *Vlas* had not been printed" (letter dated 9 July 1855, *Turgenev's Letters*, p. 67).

Nekrasov tried his hand at virtually everything: narratives, folksongs, elegies, love songs, lyrics, children's verse, satires, rhymed editorials. His complexity, diversity, unevenness—all these would make him hard enough to translate. His social concerns, very Russian and in another sense very Victorian, add yet another considerable difficulty. Nekrasov is far more of a Russian nationalist poet than is Pushkin. But Nekrasov, like Pushkin, is a great musician of the Russian language—and that is perhaps the hardest thing of all for the translator. For there is no counterpart, in our tradition; we have no sentimental social reformers who are in fact great poets, who retain anything of the clear purity of great poetic music. "Of the great Russian poets," says Sidney Monas very appropriately, "it is perhaps Nekrasov . . . who stands the least chance of assuming a viable shape in English" ("Boian and Iaroslavna," in *The Craft and Context of Translation*, p. 185). The poems here translated, accordingly, are representative of only a few aspects of his art; I find myself quite incapable of translating certain of his poems. Nekrasov's full range is simply not capturable—at least not by any one translator, and not, I think, in our time. For all that, I did make the attempt. The first eighteen lines of my abandoned translation of *Vlas*, a poem of peasant suffering and religious repentance, look like this:

> Gray-haired Vlas, in a peasant
> coat open at the neck,
> head bare, treks
> slowly through the town.
>
> A copper ikon hangs
> on his chest; he begs coins
> for a church; chains clang
> on his shoulders; his cheek is scarred;
>
> His shoes flap. His stick
> has an iron point. Once
> he'd known no God,
> sinned viciously,
>
> Beaten his wife to her grave,
> sheltered bandits
> and thieves, bought their grain
> when his neighbors needed
>
> Help, but sold for cash
> only, sold . . .

There did not seem to be much point in going on. Still, something of "the melodramatic and rugged form of Nekrasov's verse" (Slonim, *The Epic of Russian Literature*, p. 244) is represented in this book, I think, and something also of his energy and originality. (Several of the poems here translated were written during his final two years, when he was slowly dying of rectal cancer.)

Soviet criticism of course ranks Nekrasov very very high—but so too do the Russian people. His collected poetry, published in 1856, was out of print in a month; no reprint was permitted by the Tsarist censors. Even Dostoyevsky, whose early intimacy with Nekrasov had quickly given way to distant though never openly antagonistic coolness, and whose social and religious views were sharply antagonistic—even Dostoyevsky hurried to pay his last respects to the dead poet, then returned home, deeply affected, and found himself, to his own surprise, "unable to start working. I took Nekrasov's three volumes and began to read them, beginning with the first page. I sat reading all night till six o'clock in the morning, and once more I lived through those thirty years. . . . That night I read virtually two-thirds of everything Nekrasov wrote, and literally, for the first time, I understood how much Nekrasov, as a poet, had meant in my life!" (*The Diary of a Writer*, p. 936).

Self-Hate

I am in fact nothing, useless,
wasting day after ruined day.

I have never tried,
always condemned myself in advance,

Saying over and over, "I'm worthless, weak!"
Ah, how like a slave I've grovelled!

Surviving to age thirty
I've not even piled up money

So fools can grovel at my feet
and even clever people can envy me, sometimes.

I am in fact nothing, useless,
never having loved

But still wanting to love . . . . . . and loving the whole world,
wandering like a savage—homeless, with no family,

And filled with a boiling anger—
but my hand freezes whenever I reach for a knife.

Muse of Vengeance,
Muse of Sorrow

Silence, Muse of vengeance, Muse of sorrow!
Let people sleep in their beds,
we've cursed enough, you and I.
I die alone—and I die silent.

Why moan and groan, why regret what went wrong?
Ah, but if it would make things easier!
My groaning heart, squeaking like a
prison door, disgusts even me.

This is the end. These clouds, this darkness,
have come for a purpose,
the sky over my head will never turn blue,
will never warm my soul . . . . . .

Oh magic rays of love, of rebirth!
How I called you—asleep, awake,
sweating, fighting, falling into the pit,
I called and called you—but no longer!

You might light up this abyss.
I do not want to see it.
A heart weary of hate
refuses, now, to love.

I Feel So Low

Ah, I feel so low, so low,
so tired of the pain in my mind;
my tortured, butchered mind
lies so utterly drained

That somehow my heart's crazy dance
makes me ache with laughter—
if I knew it was coming, I'd go to meet
death on the way—but sleep will help—

Tomorrow I'll wake and run out the door,
greedy to greet the sun:
my soul will lift itself in delight,
and I will want to live, to live!

But this life-sucking sickness
bleeds me just the same, today, tomorrow,
and keeps telling my soul precisely
how near the dark grave has come . . . . . .

A Black Day

A black day! Like a beggar after bread
I ask for death, death,
I beg of heaven, of doctors,
of friends, enemies, even of censors,
I call to the Russian people:
if you can, come get me out of this!
Dip me in the water of life
or let me drink deep of the water of death.

Konstantine Konstantinovitch Sluchevsky: 1837–1904

SLUCHEVSKY worked for a time as clerk in a printing house; from 1891 to 1902 he served as editor of an official government newspaper. In addition to poetry he wrote novels and stories, and a good many essays and sketches.

Sluchevsky typifies that odd literary figure, the poet with a fine and well-trained mind, learned in matters scientific and philosophical, who nevertheless remains emotionally and therefore technically too unsure for his work to really develop. Like Matthew Arnold, Sluchevsky deserves fame primarily for one poem, "After an Execution in Geneva" (1880, here translated). Most of his work—like Arnold's—is flawed by ineptitudes and flatnesses, and redeemed only by phrases and passages which, instead of jarring, suddenly jell. Soviet criticism views him as a "pessimistic" and "mystical" poet, critical of "real Russian life" and deeply "bourgeois." Contemporary radicals said much the same sort of thing of Sluchevsky, just as they did of Fet—and like Fet, Sluchevsky too stopped publishing, from 1860 to 1880. In the 1880s he came out with a cycle of poems entitled "Thoughts," and with a group of poems centering on the figure of Mephistopheles. In 1902 he published *Songs from the "Corner,"* a well-received collection.

Toward the end of his life Sluchevsky became a kind of rallying point for anti-radical literary forces; he is considered a precursor of the Symbolists.

After an Execution in Geneva

Hot, grubby: time hung:
I saw an execution: a crimson scaffold
pressing on a crowd, and sun
shining on the axe.

They killed him. His head bounced like a ball!
The hangman wiped blood from his arm,
the scaffold came down like cards;
firemen hosed the square.

Hot, grubby: time hung:
I felt myself on a wheel,
torn to pieces,
bones cracked, muscles snapped—

Stretched, and stretched, and screaming
till I felt myself a string,
alive, strung
on a withered nun's

Guitar; and she plucked me, boney,
a hoarse and nasal
hag crooning "Passion Burns in My Breasts,"
and I kept time, twanging sad.

The Doll

A child throws the doll,
and it falls, it flies,
thumps on the floor with a dull
bump, and lies on its face . . . . . .
pitiful toy ! So still,
so small, so easy to break,
arms as wide as they can,
bright eyes shut—
doll, you look like a man !

Forgotten thoughts, snuffed-out emotions—
my head's poor mummies,
wrapped in death's white wool:
perhaps you're really not dead?
Silent mummies, ancient relics
of my own Egypt,
I greet you, sleeping in your quiet contemplation!
I'm here to shine a lantern for you.
Ah: yes, deep in your pyramid
you lie so quietly, you're so gentle, now;
your white coverings have blown a little
in the wind from the open door.
And you all looked up at the unexpected visitor!
Listen, mummies: tell me:
if you could be alive again—
would you do it all over? Do it differently? Yes or no?
No answer! A row of silent witnesses . . . . . .
and, of course, why should they answer?
Suppose they had:
what could I do with the knowledge? Begin all over?
Idle curiosity breeds questions
like maggots in the brain . . . . . .
The mummies, wise with age,
watch me cheerfully, but stay silent.
The lantern glitters on noiseless stone . . . . . .
and all I can feel is a final void!
A dark vault, choked with stalactites . . . . . .
turning to stone, like my heart.

Vladimir Sergeyevitch Soloviev: 1853–1900

RELIGIOUS PHILOSOPHER, Slavophile, mystic, humorist, and poet, Soloviev was the son of an eminent Moscow historian, S. M. Soloviev. After study in Russia and in London (the latter interrupted by a mystical command to go at once to Egypt, where Sophia the Divine Wisdom revealed herself to him), he was briefly a university philosophy teacher in Moscow and Saint Petersburg. He was forced from his university post, in 1881, for publicly advising the new Tsar, Alexander III, not to execute his father's assassins. Thereafter he became an active religious polemicist (and a translator of Plato); his more mystical sides were relatively private and, in the 1890s, became "less orthodox and took the form of a strange 'mystical love affair' with the Finnish Lake Saima. . . . He also had diabolical visitations" (Mirsky, *A History of Russian Literature*, p. 364).

Soloviev's poetry is much influenced by Fet, whom he knew well; Dostoyevsky is a less direct but equally powerful influence. After two hours of conversation with Dostoyevsky, Soloviev reported, "one felt as if drugged or in a state of voluptuous torment, of feverish inebriation" (Slonim, *The Epic of Russian Literature*, p. 276). Not primarily a technician, the force and cogency of Soloviev's vision made him, in turn, a prime influence on many poets, notably Blok, but also Biely, Tsvetaeva, Pasternak, and such early Symbolists as Sologub and Balmont.

Mirsky asserts that "Next to Pushkin (who has no rivals), Soloviev is no doubt the best of Russian letter writers, with Chekhov as a good third" (*A History of Russian Literature*, p. 368).

In the Alps

A powerful surf, a joyful surf
of wordless thoughts and nameless emotion . . . . . .
the rickety seawall of hope and desire
dissolves in a light blue wave.

Dark blue mountains, near,
Dark blue sea, far off.
Soul-wings rising over the earth,
but not deserting the earth.

On the shore of hope, on the shore of desire,
splashes a pearl-white wave
of a powerful surf, a joyful surf
of wordless thoughts and nameless emotion.

I Stumbled through Morning Mist

I stumbled through morning mist
toward a strange and wonderful shore.
Dawn fought with the last stars,
dreams flew in the air—and held by dreams
my soul prayed to unknown gods.

A cold white day, a lonely road,
and again I walk in some unknown land.
But the mists have gone, I can see, oh clearly,
how twisted my mountain path, how far
far away my dream still lies.

And till midnight I will walk,
unafraid, toward that lovely shore,
where high on a mountain, under new stars,
flaring with triumphant fires, I will find
my sacred temple waiting.

The World That Was

A wingless spirit, enslaved by earth,
forgotten by himself, a forgotten god ......
a dream, only a dream—and your wings
return and you fly high above worldly things.

Misty light from familiar brilliance,
faint, faint echoes of unearthly songs—
the world that was, never fading, bright,
rises slowly in front of your soul.

A dream, only a dream—and waking, heavy,
you wait with suffocating pain
for another gleam of unearthly vision,
for another echo of holy song.

Innokenty Fyodorovitch Annensky: 1856–1909

ANNENSKY WAS little known as a poet, in his lifetime. He was (like A. E. Housman) a distinguished classical scholar, and translated all the surviving plays of Euripides; he planned to, but never did, translate Plato. An accomplished linguist, he had virtually perfect fluency in German, French, Italian, and English; in addition to Latin and Greek, he had a professional command of Sanskrit and of Hebrew, and knew several Slavic languages. (His doctorate was in comparative, classic, and Slavic philology.) Annensky also translated widely from French—Leconte de Lisle, Verlaine, Mallarmé, Rimbaud, Baudelaire—as well as works of Horace, Heine, even Henry Wadsworth Longfellow. Professionally he was a teacher, for ten years headmaster of the *gymnasium* (*lycée*, or upper secondary school) at Tsarskoe Selo, residence of the Tsars, and finally Inspector of Schools for the entire Saint Petersburg district. He was returning home from work, one late fall night, when he collapsed at the train station, of a heart attack.

Annensky published a volume of lyric poems in 1904, using the pseudonym *Nik-to* ("nobody"); it was neither well received nor much noticed. His second collection, *The Cypress Chest* (named for the box in which he stored his poems), appeared posthumously, in 1910, and in 1923 his son put out a final volume, *Posthumous Verse*. From 1906 to 1909 he published two *Books of Reflections*, critical lectures which Soviet critics term, not unjustly, "impressionistic." Annensky was in fact much influenced by "impressionist/Symbolist" poets like Verlaine and Mallarmé: what Soviet critics call his "decadent," "negative" attitudes, his concern with loneliness, unhappiness, and an "unreal" beauty, are plainly symptoms of what, in the West, we call alienation. As Annensky himself put it, "But do many really understand what sort of a thing this world of ours is? For you know, during recent years, even among us, oh! how many there are who huddle around the word and are even prepared to speak about its cult. But they do not understand that the most frightening and powerful word—the most enigmatic—is perhaps just the everyday word. . . . For me there could be no more triumphant and blessed day than the one when I smash the last idol to bits. A soul that is liberated and empty, but still greedily licking its black walls like a flame —that's what I want" (quoted from V. Setchkarev, *Studies in the Life and Work of Innokentij Annenskij*, pp. 50, 52).

Although many literary histories ignore him, Annensky's influence on post-Symbolist poets has been considerable, notably his influence on Boris Pasternak. His posthumously published play, *Famira Kifared* (published in 1913, staged in 1916), anticipates Jean Giradoux and other French playwrights in its use of classical subject matter for very contemporary purposes; Annensky wrote three other tragedies, all with classical personnages and themes.

What fame Annensky had in his lifetime was largely due to his former pupil, Nikolai Gumilev, who had attended the Tsarskoe Selo school from 1903 to 1906. (Anna Akhmatova was also one of Annensky's students). Gumilev brought Annensky into Acmeist circles; Annensky also had a hand in the editing of the Acmeists' influential journal, *Apollon*.

On the Water

That, is that a meadow? A cloud? Water
bewitched by the yellow moon?
Silvery glass above me, in front of me,
in the silvery distance, behind me . . . . . .

No regret . . . . . . No desire . . . . . .
may the witch's mask gleam
and her story roll like a ball
to that silvery distance, across that silvery glass.

September

Golden gardens, rotting,
purple tinted fungus, sun's late heat
curving short, stopping
in leaves, not bottled in fruit.

And yellow silk on the ground, coarse
in places, a last meeting openly false,
and ponds black and bottomless in parks,
ripe for suffering.

But hearts sense sorrow's beauty, feel
the pull of strength all spellbound; whoever
has tasted the lotus, reels
with the insinuating breath of autumn.

After the Concert

Black clouds on the garden path,
but heart-weariness drags on . . . . . .
Lights all dark, voices vanished:
can dreams be left so wan?

Oh, her sad satin dress,
the fearful white of her breast
against the black! I pitied her still eyes,
her kid-glove submissive hands—

Ah, but the depth of soul scattered
for the indifferent, the bored, the tearless!
What lilac-soft sounds battered
in silence, spilled starlike in her fear!

Like violet sapphires on a rope
that emotion snaps,
rolling in dew-flecked grass,
in moonlight, lost without hope.

5.
From the Symbolists to the Revolution

Fyodor Sologub (pseudonym of Fyodor Kuznitch Teternikov): 1863–1927

SOLOGUB'S FATHER was a petty tradesman, his mother a domestic servant: it was her employer who helped Sologub attend a teachers' training college. Until 1907, when his superb novel, *The Little Demon*, was published, Sologub worked as a teacher and district supervisor of elementary schools. He hated the new Soviet regime, but could not bear to leave Russia: after 1917 his life became one of utter isolation. His wife, a writer and translator, committed suicide shortly before Sologub himself died.

As a poet, Sologub belonged to the Symbolists; he was the most profoundly pessimistic of the group, and has been called the most decadent. A schizoid split between the outer world and man's own consciousness shows up in almost all his work; it apparently was also reflected in his life. He once said of himself that he was "burdened by life among other people" (as quoted in Paul Miliukov, *Outlines of Russian Culture*, p. 56). His verse is graceful, craftsmanlike, melodious; its subject matter is distinctly morbid.

Sologub's work includes a collection of verse, *The Circle of Flames*, and two plays, *The Victory of Death* (1907), and *Love over the Abyss* (1914). His novels, in addition to *The Little Demon*, are *Bad Dreams* (1896), and *The Sorcery of Death* (1908–1912). All of the titles are characteristic of his intense morbidity.

My Grim Genius

Near a dusty fence,
near a heap of garbage,
down a silent street,
at the end of May
a gray Easter-root
grows, gray and unlovely.

Wandering without sense,
suffering without sense,
born in ashes,
born without brightness,
my grim genius
blooms in its pain.

Our Resurrection

Do they matter, our miserable villages? Space
and time, do they count?
Our Father has many mansions, all nameless
to us.

Heaven is real, I feel it,
but life is a dream:
I refuse its visions of sweetness,
I give back the torments of time.

Pain, and failure, and rot
are flowers for my pleasure.
Rebirth in the flesh? A promise never
to be kept, never, never.

We Can Die Together

The field is coal black.
Someone cries: Help!
But who can I help?
I am poor, and small
and tired as death:
how can I help?

And he cries in the blackness:
Brother, come to me!
Together, it is easier.
If we can't go on
we can die together, along the way,
we can die together!

Song

I like to wander along the marsh
with a trembling torch in my hand,
I like to hide like a hairy spider
in a sticky web,
I like to buzz in the meadows like a fly,
stinging horses,
I like to be the secret reason,
the only reason, for people's pain.

I am sick, vicious, mad with revenge,
but I suffer, too.
And my quiet moan, my slow midnight
howl, reproach Heaven.

Fate assigned me this rotten flesh,
this poisoned blood.
I loved, when I loved, with a prisoner's dream,
a mad love.

My pain is sinful, and everything that leads me
on, is sinful—
is a dream of many shapes,
a beautiful dream.
But the dream torments me, strikes me.
Hard! It is hard to go
my own way. I envy everyone everything
and I want to be different.

Konstantine Dmitrievitch Balmont: 1867–1943

ROMANTIC, narcissistic, immensely productive, Balmont published his first book in 1890; it has been described as traditionally melancholy. Thereafter he studied (and translated) Western writers, being particularly influenced by Shelley, Baudelaire, Whitman, and Oscar Wilde. After about 1895 his poetry became exceedingly musical, although always rather vague; from 1900 to 1905 he became a kind of Nietzschean extrovert and proclaimed himself a "revolutionary." He was extraordinarily popular, praised (and imitated) by Blok, Andrey Biely, Valery Bryusov, Bunin, Chekhov, Gorky—even the Marxist critic, A. V. Lunacharsky. Self-exiled, after the failure of the 1905 revolt, he did not return to Russia until 1913; his collected works, in ten volumes, were published between 1908 and 1913. In 1918 (asking "Am I a revolutionary?") he again exiled himself in Paris—this time for good. By 1922 he could write: "The agony of my people is strange to me; strange to me is the entire world in its struggle" (Miliukov, *Outlines of Russian Culture*, p. 76). He was written out, poor, ill—and forgotten.

With Bryusov and Sologub, Balmont was one of the three leaders of the Symbolist movement; a master of word effects, his influence—which was very real—was largely a matter of diction. He could read poetry beautifully, "like a witch-doctor," writes Ilya Ehrenburg, "who knows that his words have power, if not over evil spirits, then at least over the poor nomads who listen" (*People and Life, 1891–1921*, p. 102). His appearance was as *fin de siècle* as his verse: "As a young man, Balmont tried to commit suicide by throwing himself out of a window [there were Suicide Clubs in Russia, at the time]. He injured a leg and all his life remained slightly lame; he walked fast and looked like a hopping bird who was accustomed to fly rather than walk. His face was sometimes extremely pale, sometimes copper-colored. He had green eyes, a sparse red beard, and red hair falling in curls down his back" (ibid., p. 102). And Ehrenburg goes on: "There was about him something majestic and pitiable, arrogant and childish. . . . He loved the grandiose. . . . He wrote verse with the speed of a stenographer. . . . [But] he remained true to himself.

The revolution irritated him by its persistence: he did not want history to interfere with his life" (ibid, pp. 103–104).

A Balmont revival may be under way, at least among Slavicists outside the Soviet Union.

I Tried to Catch Shadows

I tried to catch shadows with a dream,
shadows of a day dying;
I climbed a tower and its steps trembled,
trembled under my feet.

And the higher I came the clearer I saw,
the clearer in the distance, silhouettes, outlines,
and there were sounds in the distance,
sounds from heaven, sounds from earth.

The higher I climbed the brighter the light,
the light of sleeping high mountains,
and the dying light fell like a caress,
a tender caress for my misted eyes.

And below me, below me it was night,
night on the dark still earth,
but I, I saw the sun gleaming,
gleaming and dying in the distance.

And I knew how to catch shadows,
shadows of a dying day,
and I went higher, and higher, and the steps trembled,
trembled under my feet.

The Most Subtle Colors

The most subtle colors are not in noble harmonies
but in strings
barely trembling—
they glow like planets
out past the ends of the universe,
invisible moons
never known to our earth.
And if
when we feel deeply
we do not speak, but look,
if we love without words,
we can see, we can hear,
suns shining on us,
and sparkling light
from worlds beyond worlds.

The Way of Truth

All five senses are lies. But ecstasy, but rapture
open truth to our eyes,
and without our knowing why
the dark night burns with reproach.

Down the endless twilight, deep in infinite
dreams, diamonds are born out of coal.
Truth flows higher than sense, but only revealed
when we enter the holy glow, the gleam.

Every soul holds a world of charms,
unseen—every tree hides in its greenness
an unlit fire, waiting to burn.

Touch secret powers, shake that sleeping world—
and leaping with the joy of rebirth
the unexpected will blind you with its brightness!

Chords

In the arc of a phrase
as on a mirror's still face
I discovered bits of new dreams
unknown, untold,
held
like flowers in ice.

I let them blossom,
I gave them birth
and beauty, I cracked the hard ice—
and lush lotuses breathed
like noiseless hymns
on a round glass lake.

And their silent song
and dance, circling this new
mirror, opens
a new world below the water,
half seen
in the deep, but clear, but there.

Zinaida Nikolayevna Gippius (Hippius): 1869–1945

MARRIED TO the writer Dmitri Merezhkovsky (1865–1941, whose trilogy—*The Death of the Gods*, *The Resurrection of the Gods*, and *Peter and Alexis*—was published in an inexpensive edition by the Modern Library and enjoyed a certain vogue), Gippius went with him to self-exile in Paris, after the Revolution. Much of her career is outside the scope of this book.

She was an active and often an actively unpleasant writer, fond of literary quarrels and quick with an assaulting pen. Blok, after some exposure to her and to her circle, wrote in 1914, "The Merezhkovskys I don't want to see at all. . . . I want books; from people in Petersburg I expect nothing but 'literary' discussions at best, and petty mockery or mean insinuations at worst" (quoted from Helen Muchnic, *From Gorky to Pasternak*, p. 120). Under the pseudonym "Anton Krainij," Gippius was an important contributor to several journals, among them Bryusov's *The Scales (Vessy)*. Karlinsky tells of her extended nastiness to Marina Tsvetaeva. At one point she reproached the editors of an emigré magazine for putting her poems on the same page as Tsvetaeva's —"such a conjunction," she asserted, "is in any case undoubtedly in bad taste" (Simon Karlinsky, *Marina Cvetaeva*, p. 66).

Karlinsky also speaks of her "self-centered philosophical and tragic poetry" (ibid, p. 2). One of the fairer assessments of her work is that of Annensky, who compared her poetry to "prayers addressed to nobody and asking for nothing" (quoted in Setchkarev, *The Life and Work of Innokentij Annenskij*, p. 225).

A Seamstress

For three days I've spoken to no one . . . . . .
but my mind works greedy, malicious.
My back hurts: I see
blue spots everywhere.

A church bell was droning. It stopped.
And I'm still alone with myself.
The hot-red silk squeaks and bends
under my clumsy needle.

Everything has a stamp put on it.
It's as if this thing blends into that.
Conceding this, I try to guess
that, the hidden one, the one behind.

And to me this silk is Fire.
No: not fire, now, but Blood.
And blood is only the symbol
of what our lame tongues call—Love.

Love—only a sound . . . . . . and it is too late
to tell you what comes next.
Not fire, not blood . . . . . . only satin
squeaking under a hesitant needle.

EVERYTHING AROUND US IS
slimy, awful, dirt-filled, rough,
stupid, primitive, twisted ugly,
slowly ripping, subtly corrupt,
slippery, disgusting, vulgar, packed like sardines,
smug, oh smug, slyly obscene,
heavily smiling, revoltingly craven,
a bog, a marsh, a swamp—stagnant,
not fit for life or death,
boor, slave, rotten with pus, black,
then gray, thickly gray,
dumb, dried, somnolent, vicious,
cold as a corpse, meaningless,
intolerable—fraudulent, fraudulent!

But why complain?
How cheering is a lament?
Yes, yes: it will all be different, it will all be different.

Ivan Alexeyevitch Bunin: 1870–1953

BORN OF an ancient noble family (one of his ancestors was the poet Zhukovsky's father), Bunin published his first volume of verse in 1891. He translated Romantic narratives, mostly from English: Byron's dramatic poems, for example, and Henry Wadsworth Longfellow's forgotten "classic," *The Song of Hiawatha*. Parnassian rather than Symbolist, his poetry is descriptive, realistic, delicate, basically traditional. In 1903 the Russian Academy gave him its Pushkin Prize; in 1909 he was made a member of the Academy itself. After the Revolution he emigrated to France. ("Does Bunin exist?" asked Trotsky in *Literature and Revolution*, page 23.)

Bunin won the Nobel Prize in 1933, for his prose; the award had never before gone to a Russian.

Waltz

Open lip-petals, childlike, wet,
grow cool;
the ballroom
shifts, drifts like happy songs, but slow.

Torches, candles slide in the mirror,
merge like a crystal mirage;
the ball breathes, blows
on the warm perfumed fans.

Spring

Fields steam, daylight comes white,
out on the steppe eagles scream,
their hungry cries heavy, wild
in the cold, flowing mist.

Dew on their wings, dew on the tall weeds,
fields fragrant from sleep . . . . . .
Oh Spring, your quick cold is sweet
at dawn, your lazy hunger—your call!

You have won—the steppe steams,
eagles fly high and like emperors scream,
and clouds burn with a hot fire,
and out of the mist the sun rises like a globe.

Ghosts

The dead don't die for us!
In Scotland they tell
how invisible shadows
come at midnight,

Hands mysteriously touching
harps hanging dusty on walls,
and sleeping strings wake
and sing sad, sweet songs.

Legends: we call them fairy-tales:
deaf in the daylight, not understanding day,
at twilight we live in those tales
and listen to silence, believing.

Not in ghosts, no: but we suffer
in love, are tormented in parting . . . . . .
Oh, I've heard them, and more than once,
those sad and lovely songs!

Mikhail Alexeyevitch Kuzmin: 1875–1936

POET AND EDITOR, in 1910 Kuzmin led the revolt against the Symbolists which ended in Acmeism; his 1910 manifesto, "Concerning Beautiful Clarity," was a general rallying point for neoclassicism.

Kuzmin himself was something of a Symbolist: his verse is heavily derivative, most especially of French models, and is always highly mannered. Although his work is very competent, and historically important, the *Great Soviet Encyclopedia* ignores him; Trotsky, in *Literature and Revolution* (1924), speaks of Kuzmin's work, and that of other disfavored writers (Sologub among them), as "this literature of discarded thoughts and feelings." Trotsky notes that books of poetry by these writers "have small pages and short lines, none of which are bad"; he even concedes that such poetry exhibits "quite a little art, and even an echo of once-existent feeling." Yet he concludes that "taken altogether these books are completely and entirely superfluous to a modern post-October [the date of the Bolshevik Revolution] man, like a glass bead to a soldier on the battlefield." The writers of these books are described as "internal emigrés . . . only a survival, struck with impotence" (pp. 28–29).

Much of Kuzmin's poetry was concerned with the fanatically orthodox religious sect, the Old Believers, and with erotic themes of a frequently homosexual nature. Several of his short novels—*Wings* (1907) and *Travellers by Land and Sea* (1915)—are explicitly concerned with varieties of sexual perversion.

Fujiyama in a Teacup

Tea-steam ascends, masking Mount Fujiyama,
gold volcano in a yellow sky.
How queerly landscape shrinks!
But tiny waves ripple it alive:
see thin mist clouds
broken by an ant-head sun,
and black tea-leaf birds and fish
drawing lines on quivering topaz skies!
Spring world, down in a small world:
almond tree scent, horns winding around
and around a porcelain rim swallowing a bay.
Yet a chance mimosa branch
breaks across the sky—
like a line of romantic verse
hidden in a philosophical tome.

The Pleasures of Unhappy Love

Ah, the joy of being deserted—the infinite light
gone dark! So summer
blows hard and cold, in winter—
but one remembers the sun.

A withered flower, love letters tied with a string,
laughing eyes, one or two gay times—
the road may be dark and swampy
but there was green grass, one spring.

Pleasure must learn the other roads
(deserted, broad): ah, the joy of being deserted!
But not to be loved at all:
that is the worst.

Andrey Biely (pseudonym of Boris Nikolayevitch Bugaev): 1880–1934

SON OF N. V. Bugaev, professor of mathematics at Moscow University, Biely spent eight years at the University, taking degrees in mathematics and in philosophy. His life was an unresolved series of wandering searches, both internal and physical: as Ilya Ehrenburg observed in 1919, "He is a wandering spirit that has not found a body, an unbounded torrent . . . Biely is greater and more important than his books" (*Memoirs: 1921–1941*, p. 39). At first much influenced by Soloviev, whom he met in his father's home, and by Balmont, Biely turned out verse at such a furious rate than Annensky was alarmed for him: "Heavens, when does this fellow ever think? And when does he ever get a chance to burn and destroy his creations?" (quoted from Setchkarev, *The Life and Work of Innokentij Annenskij*, p. 224). Biely did not burn much: at his death, aged only fifty-four, he had published fifty volumes—poetry, novels, essays, literary criticism, memoirs, philosophical and theoretical studies. In 1912 he discovered Rudolf Steiner and anthroposophy; from 1912 to 1916 he lived in Switzerland, at Steiner's feet. He hailed the October Revolution as the mystical rebirth of Christianity, then became disillusioned, emigrating to Berlin in 1921. In 1923 he returned, only to spend his last years in an isolation rather similar to that experienced by Boris Pasternak.

One of the leading Symbolists, Biely's career is interlocked with virtually all the great names of twentieth-century Russian literature. He was a supporter, later a close friend (and still later an imitator!) of Marina Tsvetaeva. He "discovered" Blok, introducing him both to contemporary poetry and to Russian literary circles (and later trying, with immense circuitousness, to seduce Blok's young wife). Helen Muchnic, in *From Gorky to Pasternak* (p. 120) calls him "febrile and sanctimonious," and Paul Miliukov, in *Outlines of Russian Culture* (p. 67) notes that "Biely was more artificial than natural . . . a decadent by nature." From 1904 an active contributor to Bryusov's journal, *Scales* (*Vessey*), Biely was for many years a potent critical voice. His theoretical studies, especially of Russian versification, were immensely laborious, elaborate, and mathematical, but productive more of astonished awe than of real literary results.

Biely is best known, outside of Russia, as a novelist: *The Silver Dove*, written between 1908 and 1909; *St. Petersburg*, his most famous book, written between 1910 and 1912; *Kotik Letayev*, autobiographical fiction, written between 1915 and 1916; *The Crime of Kotik Letayev*, 1922; *The Moscow Eccentric*, 1926; *Moscow Under the Blow*, 1926; *Masks*, 1932. *St. Petersburg*, in a translation by John Cournos, was published by Grove Press in 1959. Oddly, Biely's Joycean prose was most influenced by Gogol, whom he worshipped. And Biely's prose, though not his books themselves, has been immensely influential in Soviet Russian fiction.

Soviet criticism regards Biely as a deeply failed writer, mystical, pessimistic, obscurantist, reactionary. Ehrenburg is much fairer: "What dream possessed Andrey Biely when he first heard jazz? Why did he furiously take up dancing, frightening young shop-girls with his prophet's eyes? His hair had gone white at an early age; his skin was deeply tanned, and his eyes detached themselves more and more from his face, living their own life" (*Memoirs, 1921–1941*, p. 214).

Night

If there were the whisper of words,
if there were only a rooster's hard call:
meadows flattened, crushed
by the hollow unresonance of night.

Jaws open above me,
blind, open into dreamless nonexistence.
I feel their dumb power
like an awesome current.

Jaws of deep prophecy
where stars tell me my path
while whirlwinds blow.
And a frightened animal

Jumps, falls,
and its shadow leaps in front of it,
between the hills, on blue snow,
leaps light on the snow,

Down a slope,
fading under a fir tree.
Far off, a dog begins to howl,
hugs the sled, smelling wolf.

The power of fear, of legend,
of night, of space and time,
and icy dust clanging as it comes—
austere ornament of the sky.

In the Fields

The sun's antique circle,
gold, burning,
like an orange wine
flowing over a crimson river.

The earth numb
from drunkenness of air.
Gold space,
gold fields.

Sunlight lights me
down a ravine.
Black earth breaking
under my feet.

I'll run to the river,
away from Gold:
night wind cold
blows on the green meadow.

The sun's antique circle,
gold, burning,
like an orange, like wine,
runs, hides.

Into darkness,
a thin dark blue haze,
rushing all over,
falling on fields, on me, everywhere.

Life rushes into nowhere
like a dead river:
we see earth and earthly
like a heavy dull dream.

Alexander Alexandrovitch Blok: 1880–1921

More than ever I realize that to my dying day I shall never be able to adapt myself to modern life or be conquered by it. Its shameful state inspires me with disgust. Nothing could change it now—not even a revolution. With the exception of a few, humanity will rot. All that I love is art, children, and death.

ALEXANDER BLOK, 1909

BLOK's childhood was spent largely among overindulgent women, who pampered and spoiled him: he remained close to his family all his life, and had difficulty in forming other relationships. He was from the beginning moody and mystical: in 1901 he wrote that his feelings were "abstract and contrary to all mob passions." Before 1904, when he published *Poems About the Beautiful Lady*, the chief influences on his work were the lyricists Fet and Polonsky, and Vladimir Soloviev (1853–1900), the mystic and poet who incarnated the eternal feminine as, first, Sophia (wisdom), and then as the Finish lake, Saima. Blok had read widely in German Romanticism, too, especially Novalis (whose adolescent beloved, dead at age fifteen, was also named Sophie). In 1904 Blok first began to read contemporary Russian poetry, notably Bryusov and Balmont, and instead of verse based on what he had previously called "the eternal and the absolute which sooner or later all must accept," he had soon turned the ethereal Beautiful Lady into the rather vulgar Pretty Girl Friend. ("The Stranger," here translated, and written in 1906, is a stage in this process.)

His personal life then became aimless and alcoholic. The failure of the 1905 Revolution further embittered him, and by 1908 he was convinced that intellectual poetry, and its poets, had no hope of relating to the Russian people. He had already written, in a 1905 letter to his father, "I am retiring more and more . . . I shall never be a revolutionary or a 'builder of life.' . . ." After writing to his mother, in 1909, that "either one should never live in Russia, or else isolate one's self from the humiliation of partisan politics and social activities," he travelled in Europe—and applied the same dicta to all countries and cultures.

As a Symbolist, Blok was always governed by personal rather

than theoretical motivations (in contrast to, say, Biely, who made elaborate graphological studies of versification). By 1912 he felt himself entirely out of sympathy with Symbolist notions; he wrote to Biely that "we [have] passed through an epoch which lacked character. . . . Now the epoch is over." But he could find nothing meaningful around which to structure his existence, personal or poetic. On 2 January 1912 he wrote in his diary:

> When people live too long in seclusion—as for instance the Decadents of the nineties who concerned themselves only with subjects incomprehensible to the masses—and then, later on, resume their life in the world, they are lost, become helpless, and (many of them) frequently sink below the level of the masses. It has happened thus to most of us. . . . I write as one newly born. The more accustomed one is to niceties, the more disconnected become one's meditations on life. . . . Until a real connecting link is found between the transient and the everlasting, not only can one not become an intelligible writer, but one can be of no use whatsoever. (Excerpts from Blok's diary and letters which appear above and below are as cited in Paul Miliukov, *Literature in Russia*, pp. 65–67; 77.)

Much of his greatest poetry was written during this period, and shows wild oscillations, fierce and sudden swings between excited hope and deep, bitter despair.

The 1917 Revolution seemed to Blok a liberation, a realization of his dreams. In his diary for June 1917 he wrote: "No one seems to realize the fact that never before has there been in Russia such an exemplary order, and that this order is maintained with dignity and calm by the revolutionary masses. What right have we, the brains of the country, to insult by our worthless bourgeois incredulity the clever, quiet, and wise revolutionary masses?" He added, approvingly, "I should not wonder if we are killed in the name of [this] order." Never before able to cooperate with society, Blok now accepted posts in the theatrical section of the Commissariat of Education and the Commission for

Publishing the Classics; he was also a member of the Karensky government's commission to investigate the activities of Tsarist officials, and took an active part in the proceedings. Two of his greatest late poems, "The Twelve" and "The Scythians" celebrate, respectively, the Revolution as a mystical/Christian culmination (the twelve of the title are Christ's twelve disciples) and the eternally Asian nature of Russian civilization. But the bubble soon broke, and poetry seemed as meaningless as everything else; Blok died in a state of utter hopelessness.

Apart from the enormous power and grace of his poetry, Blok's greatest innovation was his "emancipation" of Russian metrics. The regular syllabic-accentual metric perfected in the eighteenth century, and used without exception thereafter, was in many of his poems shifted to a purely stress metric—a development, of course, closely paralleled in the history of English and other Western prosodies. (Blok may have been influenced, in this new metric, by the example of German poetry.)

Blok is still (Vladimir Nabokov has underlined his stature) the greatest Russian poet of the twentieth century. He is uneven, but at his best his verse burns with a haunting intensity.

The Stranger

At night heavy air
over the restaurants cuts like a knife,
spring and corruption share
echoes of alcoholic life.

And down dusty lanes,
around suburban boredom, a baker's
gilded sign fades
in the sun, a child snivels and shakes.

And every night, past
the canal, social demons with witty
tongues and rakish caps
parade along ditches: their girls are pretty.

Rowlocks creak in the park,
a woman screams, and the white moon
hangs dumb, rolls deaf in the dark,
leering like an indifferent loon.

And every night we bend
over wine, my friend and I, dazed
and still, brooding at the scent
of mysteries, dull in a violet haze.

And sleepy waiters slide
around, and drunks with rabbit eyes
pound at tables and fight
and shout "In Vino Veritas!" And I,

Every night, at the same
appointed time, I see—or dream?—
a girl in silk, framed
on a misty window screened

In fog, walking slowly
past drunks, always alone, sweeping
a breath of perfume and old
mist to a table in a corner, keeping

To herself, quiet in a feathered
hat and rustling dress, her long
hand rich with weathered
rings worn out of ancient songs.

Her magic floats to me, I stare
through a dark veil, seeing
magic everywhere,
an island, a far-off reality.

Mysteries open, a sun
is put in my hands, wine
pierces one by one
the wrinkles of my mind.

And those feathers droop
in my soul, and blue
eyes with no bottom bloom
on some faraway dune.

Someone has buried treasure
in my heart: the key is mine!
Yes, you drunken monster!
Yes, yes: truth is wine.

Comes the Commendatore

A door with a heavy curtain, windows
closed on the night. How's
your trite freedom, Don Juan,
now that fear is howling?

Elegant bedroom empty, cold;
servants asleep; blackness.
From some holy, far-off country
a cock cry echoes back.

Can a traitor hear happiness?
Life is measured in minutes.
Donna Anna is asleep, rigid,
Donna Anna is dreaming . . . . . .

The mirrors reflect, cruel,
motionless: whose face?
Is it sweet in the grave,
Anna, dreaming unworldly dreams?

There's nothing in life, no sense,
no purpose! Old Fate, go fight
your battles!—A horn blows
in the snow-filled night . . . . . .

A car flies past like an owl, splashing
light. His steps thick,
slow, the Commendatore
opens the door with a flick,

Goes in . . . . . . cold, immensely cold—
and a clock strikes, hoarse
in the dark—"You asked me
to supper." A clock. "I've come."

No answer, no answer. No sound.
An elegant bedroom full of fear;
dawn; servants sleeping;
night pale like tears.

Dawn: how cold, how weird,
when black turns thin.
Virgin of Light! Where are you, Anna—
Anna, Anna—nothing.

Only in the morning mist
the clock strikes its last knell:
Anna will rise when you're dead, Anna
will rise when you're dead, and in Hell.

Night, a Street, a Lamp

Night, a street, a lamp, a pharmacy,
light gone dim, with no sense.
Live twenty years like this:
the same. No exit: my prophecy.

First death—then the beginning, the same,
all as it was: night, frozen waves
in a dark canal, a pharmacy,
and a street, and a lamp.

The Artist

When summer burns, when winter is swept
with snow, at weddings, funerals, feasts,
I wait for a faint unknown bell
to toll for my boredom.

Here—here! Cold-eyed, I wait—
to know it, dissect it, kill it.
I wait, watchful, and it hangs in front of me,
a dim thin thread.

A whirlwind from the sea? Birds from Eden
singing in the leaves? Time stuck still?
Apple blossoms scattered like May?
An angel flying by?

Time rolls with the weight of the world.
Sound and motion, light: they expand.
History adores its face in the future.
There is no now. There is no pity, now.

And then, as a new soul struggles
to life, new forces struggle free,
like thunder a curse kills it—
reason rules.

And I take the floating, lovely bird,
flying free, flying death away,
flying souls' salvation,
and lock it in a frozen cage.

My cage: steel, heavy,
shot with gold in the dying sun.
My bird: happy, once,
now glued to a hoop, chirping in a window,

Its wings clipped, singing by rote.
You like the song, standing at my window?
My pain wears me thin, waiting
for something new, and again just bored.

Remember?

Remember? Our lazy bay
slept, water green,
when warships sailed in,
in a line.

Four, all gray. And for an hour
questions quickened us,
and sunburned sailors
strutted down the sand.

The world swelled, grew lovely,
and suddenly—off they went.
The ocean swallowed all four
of them, the ocean and the night.

And the sea turned dull again,
boring; our lighthouse blinked
sadly, after catching their last
faint semaphore signal . . . . . .

Children—you, and also me—
need so little. The heart
sings with joy at any
new toy.

Only a bit of faraway dust
on your penknife, and the world
turns strange, wrapped
in a colored mist.

Song (to Zinaida Gippius)

Born when time stood still
or rotted, you can forget.
But born of Russia's hell
we will never forget.

Time when our universe burned !
Time of insanity, or time of hope?
War time, free time, all scarred
on our faces, red as blood.

Dumb—the bells sang too loud,
we are dumb. Our hearts
clanged madly, but now, now
we are empty, dry.

Let ravens croak
our death-song—
let those better than us behold
Thy Kingdom, O my God !

Velemir (Viktor) Vladimirovitch Khlebnikov: 1885–1922

THE FOUNDING FATHER of Russian Futurism, Khlebnikov wrote his early poetry (1906–1908) under the influence of the Symbolists. An impressive reader, he gave many public recitations. His poetry began to appear in print, from 1908, and quickly declared war on virtually all aspects of traditional verse, including traditional words and traditional syntax. Poets could, he declared, and poets should invent a "transrational" (or "metalogical") language (*zaum'*, or *zaumy yazyk*), in particular constructing new words with new meanings. Perhaps his most famous poem, here translated as "Oath by Laughter," consists entirely of words constructed out of the Russian word for laughter.

Anti-Western, pagan-worshipping, Khlebnikov experimented not only with language but with elaborate mythologies, drawn from a largely imaginary Slavic past. He hailed the Revolution—and its effect on his poetry was to make it simpler, distinctly more traditional, more like Russian folk art. Some of his late poems draw fantastic pictures of a mythological Russian future.

Khlebnikov's linguistic experiments were for a time deeply influential, especially in the hectic years immediately after the Revolution, but it was Mayakovsky who was the logical culmination, as well as the height, of Futurism. Khlebnikov is today very much a poet's poet.

Oath by Laughter

Oh laughers, start laughing,
oh laughers, let's hear you laugh,
and you who laugh real laughs, who laugh laughingly and laugh
   hard,
oh start with grinning laughs,
the laughter of monstrously, incredibly laughable laughs—
the laughter of wryly laughing laughers.

Oh laugh yourself out, collapse in laughter, the laughs of
              mockingly guffawing laughsters.
Laughs—,   laughs—   :
              little grinning laughs, dry cutting laughs, hiccoughing
              laughs, tiny laughs, baby laughs, oh baby laughs.
Oh laughers, start laughing,
oh laughers, let's hear you laugh.

Song

Again, again,
I'm a star
for you.
Sailors who steer
mistaking
a star
break on the rocks,
on banks under the sea.
You've mistaken
heart's direction
from me:
you will break on the rocks
and the rocks
will laugh
as you laughed
at me.

Nikolai Stepanovitch Gumilev: 1886–1921

THE LEADER and chief theoretician of the Acmeists, Gumilev was educated in Saint Petersburg and at the Sorbonne. He began as a robust, colorful poet who loved things exotic, and of things exotic loved Africa most of all. One of his early books, *Shatyor* (*The Tent*), was devoted exclusively to poems about Africa. A Christian, though of a rather muscular sort, Gumilev believed in clarity and in action; he thought war something distinctly mystical, the natural channel for what was to him the noblest of human emotions, heroism. He was married to Anna Akhmatova, from 1910 to 1918, when she divorced him; the marriage had effectively ended in 1913.

Gumilev's energy and sensuousness make his early poetry brilliant, if sometimes shallow; his craftsmanship was always superb. He chose to return to Russia in 1917 (he had been in France, after the February Revolution, as the Provisional—Kerensky—Government's commissioner for the affairs of Russian troops). Gumilev's sympathies were monarchist and he made no attempt to conceal them: the hard, alienated last years of his life deepened and humanized his poetry. He was shot, in 1921, for anti-Bolshevik activities (of which he was quite probably guilty). It is said that he died with a cigarette in his mouth, smiling contemptuously.

Ognenny Stolp (*The Pillar of Fire*), his last and very best book, was published posthumously in 1921. Collected editions have since been published in Germany and in the United States, but not in Russia. His name does not appear in the *Great Soviet Encyclopedia:* he has become an official nonperson.

Gumilev translated Théophile Gautier, as well as Chinese and Vietnamese poetry, Coleridge's *Rime of the Ancient Mariner*, *Gilgamesh*, and Browning's *Pippa Passes*. He wrote some perceptive literary criticism, some interesting short stories, and a number of plays, including a play for children, *The Tree of Transformation*, which was staged in 1918. A major mover in the Leningrad Poets' Guild, Gumilev was a dedicated teacher of young poets; he was almost religiously convinced that anyone could learn to write respectable poetry.

The Selected Works of Nikolai S. Gumilev, translated by Alla Burago and myself, will appear shortly. It will be volume 1 in a series, Russian Literature in Translation, under the general editorship of Sidney Monas, to be published by the State University of New York Press.

The Sixth Sense

Fine is the wine that loves us,
and the bread baked for our sake,
and the woman who lies and loves us
when she's finished her tweaking games.

But sunset clouds, rose
in a sky turned cold,
calm like some other earth?
Immortal poems?

All inedible, nonpotable, unkissable.
Time comes, time goes,
and we wring our hands
and never decide, never touch the circle.

Like a boy forgetting his games
and watching girls in the river
and knowing nothing but eaten
by desires stranger

Than he knows—like a slippery creature
sensing unformed wings
on its back and howling helpless
in the bushes and brambles—like hundred

Years after hundred years—how long, Lord,
how long?—as nature and art
cut, and we scream, and slowly, slowly
our sixth-sense organ is surgically born.

A Workman

A red-glowing forge, a small
old man, standing;
red eyelids blinking
and his face submissive, calm.

The others are asleep,
he's alone, busy
casting the bullet that will cut me
away from the earth.

Done—and his eyes grow gayer.
He goes home. The moon is shining;
his wife, sleepy and warm,
lies waiting in a big bed.

His bullet will whistle
across this Russian river,
will find my heart.
It has come to find me.

I will fall, twisting, I will see
history as history was,
while my blood will rush
like a fountain on the dusty, beaten grass.

And the Lord will reward me, yea
in full, for this swift and bitter
life. And this was done by the small
old man in the faded grey blouse.

The Lost Tram

A strange street, then crows
croaking, then the sound of a lute
and thunder crawling slow
from a distance—then a tram at my feet

And I leaped, somehow, and the railing
held, and I stood, dazed,
stupidly watching a trail
of fire streaking like sun-rays.

Rushing like a storm with dark wings
the tram blundered and was lost
in time's pit . . . . . . "Driver, off!
Stop! This minute—listen!"

No. We'd run round the wall,
plowed a palm grove, clattered
a Neva bridge, a Nile
bridge, a bridge on the Seine,

And seen for a second a beggar
watching with knowing eyes—
the beggar from Beirut, right,
the same: he died

Last year. Where am I? My heart
pumps languid fear: "Did you miss
the station? They sell tickets there
for the India of the Spirit."

A sign . . . . . . bloody letters
spelling Grocer: better
than turnips or beets they sell
bleeding heads, severed.

The butcher with a face like an udder
and a red shirt takes my head
too and slops it in a box
of heads, at the bottom.

A side street, house with three windows,
wooden fence, a lawn . . . . . .
"Driver, I need to get down
here, stop, this minute!"

Mashenka: you lived here, and sang,
and wove me a rug, and promised
to marry me. Body and voice
where are you? Not dead, not you?

You moaned in your room when I powdered
my hair to present myself
to the Empress. I never
saw you again.

I see: freedom for us
is light from another world;
men and shadows wait
at the gate of the planet's zoo.

And then a sweet familiar
wind, and over that bridge
an iron glove and two hooves
rush toward me.

Saint Isaac's dome on the sky
like God's true hand:
let them sing for Mashenka
and mourn for me.

How can I breathe? It hurts
to live. My heart tears
itself. Mashenka, I never knew
how much love and sorrow we can bear.

Anna Akhmatova (pseudonym of Anna Andreyevna Gorenko): 1888–1966

AKHMATOVA was born in Kiev; her father was a merchant marine officer. She was married, in 1910, to Nikolai Gumilev, leader of the Acmeists. They had one child, a son.

Akhmatova began her poetic career as a miniaturist, with the clear, rather quiet and conversational lyrics of *Chotki* (*Beads*, 1914; see "Evening" and "I Think of You Now and Then," here translated). During and after World War I her poems became more severe ("July, 1914," here translated). By the time of *Anno Domini* (1922), she was writing with the weight and precision of her fully matured, distinctly classical style ("Everything Is Stolen," here translated; the poem was written in 1921).

She divorced Gumilev in 1918; their marriage had broken up in 1913.

Akhmatova's *Iva* (Willow Tree, 1940) and especially her greatest book, *Poema Bez Geroya* (*Poem Without a Hero*, written between 1940 and 1943 but not published until 1960, and then in New York, not in Russia), do not come within the scope of this book. It is her later work, in particular, which earned her the reputation of the greatest of living Russian poets—even though it was difficult for her to publish her work while Stalin was alive. (She was in fact expelled from the Writer's Union, in 1946.)

Evening

Music in the garden sings
sadder than words;
sea-smells rise, sharp,
from oysters on a plate of ice.

"I'm a faithful friend," he says,
touching my dress.
How different from the touch of love,
the motion of those hands!

You pat a bird, like that,
a cat; you stare at handsome acrobats,
like that. His quiet eyes just laugh
under gold furred lashes.

And sad violins sing
through the smoke:
"Thank God, thank God: you're alone at last
with the man you love."

I Think of You Now and Then

I think of you now and then;
your path does not interest me;
but that casual meeting
has marked my soul.

I walk by your house, red
above the muddy river,
knowing I break your sunbaked
peace.

Someone else bent toward my lips,
hungry for love,
someone else spun my yearning
into infinite golden poems—

But when the evenings turn blue
I throw spells over the future,
and I know we will meet again,
we will have to.

July, 1914

1)

Burning, smoke and smell:
peat bogs flaming all month.
No birds sing,
aspens no longer tremble.

Sun like God's displeasure:
no rain since Easter.
A priest with one leg
stands in the courtyard, saying:

"Days will be bad. Our soil
will open with graves.
Expect starvation, plagues, earthquakes,
stars snuffed out.

"But the enemy will not enjoy himself,
chopping our country apart:
the Mother of God will cover us
with a white veil."

2)

Odor of juniper from burning forests.
Soldiers' wives moan,
holding their children;
widows weep.

But prayers have power,
the earth melts dry, longing
for rain, and hard-packed fields
have showers of warm red wetness.

The bare sky hangs low, low,
prayers are almost whispered:
"They are piercing Your holy body,
they are gambling for Your clothes."

Everything Is Stolen

Everything is stolen, sold, betrayed;
Death's black wing flags across us;
everything is gnawed by pain—
and why is there light?

The sun on a strange forest
breathes a flavor of cherries;
stars shine in the clear summer
night like new constellations;

And the broken, dirty houses
feel miracles closer, closer—
miracles never known,
longed for from the beginning of time.

Boris Leonidovitch Pasternak: 1890–1960

SON OF a well-known painter, Pasternak began by studying music, and later—both in Russia and in Germany—philosophy. Although never attracted to movements or ideologies of any kind (Ehrenburg, *People and Life*, *1891–1921*, p. 280, records that "Pasternak said many times that he could not understand the various trends and schools"), he felt a bond with the Futurists. Mayakovsky was for some years his particular idol, though their personal relationship was stormy. He published his first book of poems in 1913, a second in 1917; in 1921 he published *Sestra Moya Zhizn'* (*My Sister, Life*), consisting of poems written in 1917, and was hailed as a major writer. It was also recognized that Pasternak neither belonged to nor was likely ever to belong to any literary school: his manner, as well as his voice, was entirely his own.

Most of Pasternak's career, both as poet and as translator, is outside the scope of this book. I have, however, translated one late poem, "Hamlet" (it was included in *Doctor Zhivago*, 1957), as well as one early poem, for the simple reason that Pasternak's early poetry does not do him justice. He has become a substantial figure in world literature: his stature seems to demand this minor relaxation of chronological boundaries.

Pasternak was awarded, but not allowed to accept, the Nobel Prize for 1958.

In a Wood

Meadows blurred in the mauve heat,
in the woods cathedral-darkness expanded.
Was there anything left to kiss?
It was theirs, all of it, soft as warm candles.

A dream: not sleep, but longing
for sleep; someone almost asleep
and under his eyelids a pair of black suns
charring at his lashes, as he sleeps.

Sun, and shining beetles;
dragon-flies graze his cheeks.
Tiny vibrations all through the forest—
like trees in a watchmaker's tweezers.

He dozed while numbers ticked; over
his head, amber, harsh, a perfect-
wound clock shifted its calibrations
to balance the heat.

Clock adjusted; pine needles shaken;
shadows blown, tree trunks worn,
skewered like a weary day,
mounted on the clock's blue form.

Ancient happiness sinking,
woods swamped in a sunset
of dreams. Happiness ignores clocks—
but these two only slept.

233

Hamlet

They're quiet. I mount the stage.
Leaning on an open door
I strain at an echo, far off,
hunting what the future is for.

The rim of night shines back at me
from a thousand peering glasses.
If You can, Abba, Father,
let this cup be passed

Away from me. I adore Your stubborn plan,
I will smile and read the lines.
But tonight it's a different script
so excuse me, please, this time.

Yet scene must follow scene, the road
goes where it goes. I'm alone, everything
drowns in a pious show.
Life is no casual jingle.

Osip Emilievitch Mandelstam 1891–1938(?)

ONE OF the Acmeists, Mandelstam was steeped in Latin and Greek poetry; his attitudes, the structure of his verse, even his Russian, bear the mark of his classical training. He studied in Paris, 1907, and in Heidelburg (where he worked at Old French). His first published poem appeared, in 1910, in the journal *Apollon*. In 1913 he published his first book, *Kamen'* (*Stone*), at his own expense. *Tristia* (1922) was the second and also the last collection of his verse, though later poems appeared in periodicals and, in the 1960s, the verse of his prison years was published (though not in Russia).

Mandelstam was small, frail, odd looking; meeting him in Paris, in 1907, Roman Jakobson, the emigré linguist, found him compelling, but noted that he looked very like a chicken. The contrast between his intense seriousness about literature, and his relatively innocent (some called it frivolous) attitude toward most other things, was frequently commented on. "His poems were born out of a line, a single word; he altered everything hundreds of times. . . . The gestation period for an eight-line poem was long—sometimes it took months—and he was always overwhelmed by the birth of a poem" (Ehrenburg, *People and Life, 1891–1921,* p. 340). Mandelstam's innocence cost him his life. In 1934, probably in Boris Pasternak's apartment, he read an epigram on Stalin to a very small group of friends, one of whom, himself in fear of the secret police, betrayed him. In May he was arrested and, after a personal interrogation by Stalin himself, was exiled for three years. Released in 1937, but with his health already deteriorated, he was rearrested in 1938, and this time was sentenced to five years. He died, says Clarence Brown (translator of *The Prose of Osip Mandelstam*) in 1938, at the camp near Vladivostok where he was a political prisoner.

Mandelstam wrote a good deal of excellent prose; he translated from French and from English; and he wrote, between 1920 and 1926, three books of poetry for children.

The Complete Poetry of Osip E. Mandelstam, translated by Alla Burago and myself, is in progress and will probably appear in 1972.

Insomnia. Homer. Sails stretched taut.
A flock of ships, and I've counted
half its length: cranes
that floated over Greece.

A wedge of cranes in the distance—
crowned heads covered with god-foam—
sailing where? Without Helen
would you think of Troy, O Greeks?

Homer. The sea. Love moves everything.
Can I listen? Not Homer, now;
he is still. And the black sea shouts
near my pillow, crashes and roars.

Orioles Sing in Trees

Orioles sing in trees, and metrical
verse is measured in vowels.
Once a year Nature has quantity
too, like Homer's lines.

A day, that day, cavernous like a caesura:
peaceful, sluggish; ox at the grass,
air too heavy to be blown through a reed
for as long as a single full note.

Petropolis Dying

A light drifting terribly high,
glittering brighter than a star:
O transparent star, drifting light,
your brother, the city of Peter, is dying.

At that terrible height earth-dreams
burn, and a green star glitters.
O star, if sky and water are your brothers,
your brother, the city of Peter, is dying.

At that terrible height a phantom ship
spreads huge wings, and flies!
O green star, ruined and beautiful,
your brother, the city of Peter, is dying.

The thin spring cracks, above the black Neva,
and infinity is melting.
O star, if you are the city of Peter,
your brother, the city of Peter, is dying.

Marina Ivanovna Tsvetaeva: 1892–1941

TSVETAEVA'S GRANDFATHER was a noted historian, her father a professor of art. She was educated partly in Russia, partly abroad (Switzerland, France, Germany): as a child she wrote verse in both Russian and German. Dramatic and vastly energetic in person, her poetry too is sweeping, high-pitched. Although she began to publish as early as 1910, her best verse appeared from 1922 on; her first two books included much poetry written while she was still a schoolgirl.

Tsvetaeva's career is mostly outside the scope of this book. The almost hysterical quality of her poem, "Our Lady Freedom" (written in 1917), was apparently motivated in good part by her husband's decision to join the White Army. Simon Karlinsky (*Marina Cvetaeva*, p. 8) points out that "the autobiographical element played a major role in everything [she] wrote." He adds (ibid., p. 41): "Her notion of rebellion was heroic and individualistic; her favorite heroes were the ones who raise themselves high above the crowd only to be ultimately vanquished by mediocrities. . . . There was nothing like this in the colorless politicians and dusty troops of the early days of the February Revolution." After the October (Bolshevik) coup, her antipathy became stronger still: drunken rioting seemed to her typical of Russia's new ruling class.

Tsvetaeva joined her husband abroad, in 1922. After years of grinding poverty, and fierce homesickness, the entire family returned to Russia in 1939, whereupon her husband was arrested and executed, her oldest daughter was arrested (her second daughter had died of starvation before Tsvetaeva went into exile), her son was taken into the army and soon killed in action, and Tsvetaeva herself was banished to a provincial region where she could find no work and suffered immense hardships. She hanged herself in 1941.

In addition to a number of quite long poems, Tsvetaeva wrote three plays—*The End of Casanova*, *Theseus*, and *Phaedra*—which have never been staged.

Variations on a Folksong Theme

If fate threw us together, you
and me, oh how the world would dance!
City after city would bow itself down,
oh my own, my brother-in-soul!

As soon as the last light went out
the tavern queen would be me, the king
would be you: bow, bow, to my king!
Bow to his queen!—My gift to you all: is me.

If fate threw us together, you
and me, the Tsar would ring out bells;
all down the Moscow River
bells for the beautiful fraud and her friend.

And after the ball, the dance, the feast,
we'd roll along the night wind, my brother . . . . . .
dust would fly from the road—the white, white
road—if fate would throw us together!

And the Poems I Wrote

And the poems I wrote, so young, so young,
not even knowing I was a poet,
poems that ripped off like a fountain splashing,
like sparks from a rocket,

Poems that ripped, like devils, tiny devils,
right inside, to where dreams and incense lie,
oh my poems about being young and about death
—my unread poems!—

Sprinkled in dusty closet-shops
(where no one went, and where no one finds them, now!) . . . . . .
my poems, like rare, expensive wine,
will have their turn.

TSVETAEVA   For Anna Akhmatova

The marketplace, people shouting,
steam floating from a bakery.
I remember a haggard street-singer
with a crimson mouth.

Wearing a flower-petalled kerchief
(may your prayers be answered),
standing eyes turned down,
in a crowd of women at a monastery gate,

Pray for me, too, oh
sorrowful, hell-burned beauty,
when the forest-dwelling dissenters
elect you Our Lady of the Flagellants.

Our Lady Freedom

You stepped from a Grecian church, severe
and silent, to hysteria in public squares:
freedom!—the Lovely Lady of dukes
and Russian princes.

The savage choir will sing
another moment—then the Liturgy!
Freedom!—A whore lying
in a soldier's hot arms!

List of Works Cited

BELINSKY, VISSARION. "Thoughts and Notes on Russian Literature," in *Belinsky, Chernyshevsky, and Dobrolyubov: Selected Crticism*. Edited by Ralph E. Matlaw. New York: E. P. Dutton & Co., 1962.

DANIELS, GUY. *A Lermontov Reader*. New York: Macmillan Co., 1965.

DOSTOYEVSKY, FYODOR. *The Brothers Karamazov*. Translated by Constance Garnett. New York: The Modern Library, 1950.

———. *The Diary of a Writer*. New York: Charles Scribner's Sons, 1949.

EHRENBURG, ILYA. *People and Life, 1891–1921*. New York: Alfred A. Knopf, 1962.

———. *Memoirs: 1921–1941*. New York: World Publishing Co., 1964.

GINZBURG, EVGENIA S. *Into the Whirlwind*. London: Penguin Books, 1968.

GORKY, MAXIM. *Reminiscences of Tolstoy, Chekhov, and Andreyev*. New York: The Viking Press, 1959.

HARE, RICHARD. *Pioneers of Russian Social Thought*. 2d ed. New York: Vintage Books, 1964.

KARLINSKY, SIMON. *Marina Cvetaeva*. Berkeley: University of California Press, 1966.

LERMONTOV, MIKHAIL YURIEVITCH. *A Hero of Our Time*. Translated by Vladimir Nabokov. New York: Anchor Books, 1958.

MANDELSTAM, OSIP. *The Prose of Osip Mandelstam*. Translated by Clarence Brown. Princeton: Princeton University Press, 1965.

MASLENIKOV, OLEG. "Russian Literature from 1890–1917," in *A Handbook of Slavic Studies*. Edited by Leonid I. Strakhovsky. Cambridge: Harvard University Press, 1949.

MATTHEWS, JACKSON. "Third Thoughts on Translating Poetry," in *On Translation*. Edited by Reuben A. Brower. New York: Oxford University Press, 1966.

MERESEREAU, JOHN, JR. *Baron Delvig's Northern Flowers 1825–1832: Literary Almanac of the Pushkin Pleiad*. Carbondale, Ill.: Southern Illinois University Press, 1967.

MILIUKOV, PAUL. *Literature in Russia*. New York: A. S. Barnes & Co., 1960.

MIRSKY, D. S. *A History of Russian Literature, from Its Beginnings to 1900*. Edited by F. J. Whitfeld. New York: Vintage Books, 1958.

———. *Pushkin*. New York: E. P. Dutton & Co., 1963.

MONAS, SIDNEY. "Boian and Iaroslavna," in *The Craft and Context of Translation*. Edited by William Arrowsmith and Roger Shattuck. New York: Anchor Books, 1964.

———. *The Third Section: Police and Society in Russia under Nicholas I*. Cambridge: Harvard University Press, 1961.

MUCHNIC, HELEN. *From Gorky to Pasternak*. New York: Random House, 1961.